SPONTANEOUS BRILLIANCE

Unleash the Power of Your Unique Creative Genius

SPONTANEOUS BRILLIANCE

Unleash the Power of Your Unique Creative Genius

By
SANDRA CAVANAUGH

Edited by: Vicki Anne Crane, Michele Chynoweth, and Michelle Oneida
Cover Design: Miguel Ayela
Cover Editor: Lanh Russell
Photograph of Author: Brittni Oneida

First edition October 2022
ISBN 979-8-9875778-9-9
eBook ISBN 979-8-9875778-8-2
Audiobook ISBN 979-8-9875778-7-5

Published by Miracle Publishing Group
www.miraclepublishinggroup.com

For Rex
There is no why
and
Now I know why

For Oly
This is me, finally holding onto the ball

For Mom
For everything

TABLE OF CONTENTS

INTRODUCTION
THE BRILLIANT TRUTH

Some part of you knows you are brilliant. You may not believe it or understand it or even recognize it fully, but deep inside, you can feel it! And that's why we're here. We are here to bring that feeling — that little whisper of possibility — into glorious expression, which is exactly why I wrote this book.

This is me, personally, asking you to consider the possibility that you are so much more than you have allowed yourself to be. I need you to know that you are, without a doubt, a unique creative genius bursting with brilliant, valuable, powerful thoughts and ideas.

Because here is the brilliant truth:

Whether you believe it or not (frankly, whether anyone believes it or not), the fact is that everyone — and I do mean everyone — is brilliant. Each and every person on this planet is a unique creative genius in their own right.

The problem with brilliance is not that some people have it and some people don't. The problem is that relatively few people live, learn, or work in the proper circumstances for that brilliance to be expressed. Simply put, there is no shortage of brilliance on this planet, just a reluctance to offer it and a resistance to accepting it.

Let's be honest, when was the last time you looked at yourself in the mirror and knew that you were looking at a genius? When was the last time you looked around and believed that everyone you could see, regardless of their age, education, occupation, or limitation, was a uniquely brilliant, creative genius? If your answer is never, don't feel bad. Given what we think we know about genius, most people would agree with you.

For instance, we believe that there are people who are brilliant and people who are not. We believe there are creative people and non-creative people. We believe that there are those with talent and those without. We believe that there are relatively few geniuses and a lot of non-geniuses.

Somewhere along the line, we bought into this notion that the cosmic lottery favors some of us more than others. We have come to accept that the rare few brilliant, creative geniuses move to the forefront of life. They are the ones who make all of the discoveries and innovations that solve problems and fill needs for the rest of us, while we just exist in the background somewhere, providing the backdrop for their brilliance.

And the good news is that we are wrong.

The simple fact is that none of us belong in the background of someone else's life. We each belong in the foreground of our own life. We belong center stage!

Each of us is a unique creative genius with a powerful purpose that we came here to share. Let me state that another way (in case you missed it the first time): *You* are a unique creative genius with a powerful purpose that you came here to share!

We each have a responsibility to ourselves and to the world to do, speak, share, and create what we came here for. Unfortunately, most of us spend our lives hiding in plain sight, never having our genius, our passion, or our gifts fully realized by the world, or even by ourselves.

But it's not a matter of lacking brilliance. We have the product; it's just a delivery problem. And that's where this book comes in.

I'm going to take you on a fun and festive journey through what I like to call my "metaphorical, metaphysical guide to life."

We're going to break through some long-held myths and misunderstandings and we're going to explore some spontaneous, simple, playful ways to:

- reignite your sense of playfulness and wonder
- recognize and honor your own brilliance
- think, decide, and act with clarity and confidence
- step to center stage in your own life
- show the world the magnificent, unique creative genius that is you

I believe in you.

Now it's time for you to believe in yourself.

Here we go.

CHAPTER 1

THE METAPHORICAL, METAPHYSICAL GUIDE TO LIFE

"Everybody is a genius. But if you judge a fish by its ability to climb a tree, it will live its whole life believing that it is stupid."

- **Albert Einstein**

UNIVERSALLY ACCEPTED GENIUS

Perhaps the most famous, documented, universally accepted genius is Albert Einstein. His name has literally become synonymous with the word genius. If I call you an Einstein, you know that I'm essentially calling you brilliant. Yet Albert Einstein is the same person whose slow verbal development led his parents to seek the help of doctors, and whose rebellious nature in school resulted in one headmaster expelling him and another stating that he would never amount to anything.

We love knowing in retrospect that his genius was hiding in plain sight the whole time. We enjoy the fact that they were so very wrong.

There was nothing wrong with Little Albert, there was only something wrong with the way in which his abilities were being assessed and judged. The people around him were not accurately assessing his ability to learn or to create. They were judging his capacity for brilliance based on what they thought he should be doing. His parents didn't understand that Little Albert, the silent preschooler, was so busy thinking, seeing, and noticing that he didn't talk. The teachers didn't understand that, as a young student, he was so caught up in his thoughts about math and science that he simply did not want to take time out to study the other subjects.

Just think about this for a moment. Can you imagine our lexicon, not to mention the many areas of mathematics and science, without the contributions of our friend Mr. Einstein? If he had not offered his ideas to the world, had kept them to himself, continued to quietly think rather than offer his thoughts, and accepted the labels and judgements placed on him, responding as though they were true, the world would have assumed that he didn't say anything simply because he didn't have anything to say.

Fortunately for us, despite the early feedback that Einstein received, he was still able to notice his own brilliant, creative genius. And then came the best part: he nurtured it, he explored it, he played with it, he applied it, he developed it, he persisted with it, he offered it, and we accepted it!

So here's what we need to understand: Einstein was not a singular or special case because he *was* a genius. He was singular and special because he was able to *share* his unique genius.

EINSTEIN AGREES

Everyone is brilliant at something. At *their* thing.

The reason we have trouble accepting that as a fact is because we are all used to our brilliance being assessed incorrectly, going unrecognized, or worse yet, being shut down. We don't know how to recognize, explore, nurture, and share our genius as Einstein did.

Regardless of whether it's hidden or expressed, the fact still remains that every single one of us is a unique creative genius.

You might still be thinking: "Einstein's genius was a remarkable thing! It was singular! It was special! It was unique!" And I agree with you! His genius was special and unique. I'm not disputing that. All I'm saying is *so is yours*.

But, if you don't believe me, perhaps you'll believe the man whose name has become synonymous with genius. Yes, it's true. Einstein himself also believed that *everyone* is a genius. How do we know that he did? Because he said so.

EINSTEIN'S METAPHOR

"Everybody is a genius. But if you judge a fish by its ability to climb a tree, it will live its whole life believing that it is stupid."

- Albert Einstein

And that, my friend, is why most of us don't believe that we, or the people around us, are geniuses. We've been living in a world where the only accepted demonstration of genius is to climb the tree (metaphorically speaking). But what if we were not born to climb trees? What if we were born, as most of us were, for something else?

I love metaphors. Einstein's metaphor of the fish and the tree is, in fact, my second favorite metaphor. And as any of my students, clients, or probably anyone who has ever heard me speak for more than five minutes will tell you, I not only love metaphors, I *love* to play with them and extend them *a lot*.

So let's do that with this one, shall we?

EXTENDING THE METAPHOR

Let's suppose for a moment that, once upon a time, some very well-meaning monkeys who were super great at climbing trees noticed that some of the other monkeys were not as good at climbing trees. So, in an attempt to share their success, they developed a system for climbing trees in what they considered to be the "best" way. Their intention was to help themselves and all monkeys to get better and better at climbing, and in doing so, become better and better at their overall monkey-ness.

The well-meaning monkeys who created the system acquired a lot of data to support their system. Of course, the data didn't assess the relative happiness of the monkeys or whether or not all monkeys were even interested in getting better and faster at climbing trees. The data measured success within the system and the data clearly showed that the majority of monkeys improved in their climbing skills within the system. The system became accepted, more practiced, and more valued until it was eventually seen to be responsible for every tree climbing success had by every individual monkey. Success was graded and recorded, competition was encouraged, and those that were most successful at the system were rewarded. And as better, faster climbing became synonymous with better monkey-ness, the system became sacred.

Of course, being compassionate beings, the well-meaning monkeys wanted everyone to be as successful as they were! So they shared the system with all the creatures in the land. They collected new data that now not only judged monkeys, but also the proverbial fish as well as lions, sharks, whales, elephants, giraffes, birds, and all the rest, on their ability to climb trees.

It never occurred to the well-meaning monkeys that the system was not based on the goals, strengths, aptitudes, and desires of these other creatures. They never considered that the system might be flawed, they only pitied the creatures who were too flawed to benefit from the system.

As the well-meaning monkeys saw the other creatures struggle, they didn't give up on their fellow beings' ability to be more like them, oh no! They developed supports and accommodations to compensate for the poor unfortunate creatures' lack of monkey-ness. And it still never occurred to any of them that their precious system may actually be harming the very creatures they were trying so hard to save.

But if, as our fellow genius Einstein imagined, you happen to have been born a fish, then not only are you not going to be able to climb the tree, but every moment you spend in the waterless, monkey-friendly environment is literally killing you. And the tragic misconception that the monkeys came to believe was as follows: As you die in the system, the system didn't fail you, you failed the system because you didn't climb the tree.

FLIPPING THE METAPHOR

Now let's suppose, just for a moment, that we flipped the situation upside down. What if we went from a system based on competition to one of cooperation and collaboration, valuing each creature for the special, unique attributes they were born with? What if we let the giraffe or the bird show the monkeys how fast they can access the top of the tree? They could do it faster and, perhaps in some instances, better than even the best monkey. Seems logical. But this radical idea blows the monkeys' circuits because, after all, isn't climbing the point? If the bird flies up there or the giraffe extends its neck, does it really count?

And what would happen to the perspective of the well-meaning monkeys if we flipped the situation a bit more aggressively? What if we insisted that monkeys experience being part of a non-monkey system, say, by asking a monkey to reach the top of the tree without using its hands or feet? It wouldn't be able to, but a giraffe could. What if we asked a monkey to get to the top of the tree without touching it in any way? It could not, but a bird could. And if we took the tree entirely out of the equation and asked a monkey to survive for ten minutes underwater...

You get the picture.

The point is that there is no more reason for a fish to be labeled stupid because it can't climb a tree than there is for a monkey to feel failure because it can't breathe under water. There is nothing wrong with the monkey. It has wonderful, unique, perfect gifts, just not the breathing under water one.

THE REAL PROBLEM

Our fellow genius Mr. Einstein's point was that the real problem is not a lack of ability on the part of the fish. The problem is one of perception and expectation. The problem resides within the system itself and the expectations that we have learned from it.

There are many educational scholars, developmental specialists, and creativity gurus out there railing about the failings in our educational systems in virtually every country in the world, and I'm heartened by the recognition that something has to change. But even though the system is broken, the real problem is in our thinking. Our thinking about creativity, imagination, talent, intelligence, and genius is so backwards and broken that we can't change for the better until we change our thinking.

To quote Mr. Einstein one more time:

> *"A serious problem cannot be solved at the same level of thinking that created it."*

The issue is not that the system is broken, it's that we can't or won't think outside the box we've created in order to devise how to fix our perspective on ourselves and each other.

SILLY MONKEYS

Nobody reading this actually thinks that the metaphorical situation where every creature in nature is judged on their monkey-ness would really happen. We know that each creature on earth simply does what they were born to do. Fish aren't judged on which monkey things they can or cannot do. Fish don't worry about being more like a monkey and they don't think that something went wrong in nature because they aren't a monkey. Fish don't swim around taking tests to see which one of them is most like a monkey or even which one is the smartest, best fish. Of course they don't. That would be silly. Only humans do that.

Only humans think that they are smarter than nature, smarter than the Universe. Only humans seem to believe that the cosmic lottery is something we randomly, or not so randomly, win or lose, and we just have to accept it either way.

We pick the ones that we believe the Creator did a good job on and then with the rest of the humans, the ones where the Creator blew it, we set about trying to fix them. Fixing them means making them more like the ones we deemed to be created correctly. But what if — just what if — we were each created perfectly, individually, and uniquely for whatever we were born to be and do?

RESHAPING OUR THINKING

Just as the monkey may not see the value in swimming like a fish until the moment it is under water, we may not understand or value the inherent brilliance in each other. But if we can teach ourselves to behave as if we believe it's there, then the world will completely change for us in that moment. With just a few simple shifts in our understanding and our behavior, we can step into a world of unlimited possibilities as we learn to expect and respect the inherent brilliance in ourselves and in each other.

To quote the little elf Judy in the movie *The Santa Clause* (1994):

"Seeing isn't believing. Believing is seeing."

Or as a special education teacher I once worked with said to a room full of highly engaged students with cognitive and behavioral disabilities:

"You know what I love about Ms. Cavanaugh?
She teaches like she doesn't know there is anything
you can't do... and so there isn't."

I have made a career and a life out of expecting brilliance from everyone and given the opportunity, ten times out of ten, I find it. I have had tremendous success with people of all ages and abilities, bringing out their creative genius that, oftentimes, they themselves didn't even suspect existed. In 35 plus years, I have never met a person I couldn't get to express their brilliance in some previously unimagined way.

I didn't make them brilliant — they already *were*! I just gave them the tools they needed to express it and I held the faith until they were able to themselves. With every single person, it's about them being able to offer their brilliance and the rest of us being willing to accept it. We just need to live each day knowing that each of us is a unique creative genius, accepting that as fact, and acting accordingly. It's simple.

I know what you're thinking. *"OK, that's nice, but there's just one problem: it's totally unrealistic! Wait, scratch unrealistic, it sounds downright **impossible**!!! How can you say it's **simple**? How are we supposed to change the deeply ingrained, systemic patterns, practices, and beliefs that we've spent our lifetimes conforming to **simply** by picking them apart using Einstein's metaphor?!"*

Relax. Not to worry. That's why Einstein's metaphor is my second favorite!

MY FAVORITE METAPHOR

"All the world's a stage and all the men and women merely players."

- William Shakespeare, *As You Like It* (2.7.138)

For three decades of teaching acting and improvisation, I heard myself saying to students time and time again: *"In acting, as in life… [insert wisdom here],"* or *"In improvisation, as in life… [insert wisdom here]."* Eventually, I gave up thinking it was just a marvelous coincidence and started accepting it as an essential truth: acting and improvisation are direct metaphorical explorations of the fundamentals of life.

I realize it's not a revolutionary concept to recognize the usefulness of improvisation and acting technique in nonperformance circumstances. Theater games and improv games have been used to teach communication, confidence, leadership, and team building in corporate retreats and HR workshops for decades, often to the fearful chagrin of the participants. Yes, the techniques are helpful and useful in building self-esteem and communication, but that is just scratching the surface.

You see, Shakespeare didn't just drop a nice little poetic metaphor on us, he wrote a one sentence lesson plan for life! All the world's a stage is not a fanciful parallel, it's actually a literal comparison. Each and every fundamental concept or technique that solves a problem in the pursuit of successful acting or improvisation does exactly the same thing when utilized on the great stage of life.

Shakespeare's quote is a highly spiritual metaphor, "meta" being the operative part of that word. It gives the foundation for a meta view of what we are doing here and how we can be most successful at going about it. "All the world's a stage" is what I call a metaphorical, metaphysical guide to life.

METAPHOR IN MOTION

By now you know that I love nothing more than to extend a metaphor. Spoiler alert! That is what the rest of this book is: a detailed metaphorical roadmap to successfully navigating the role you have chosen to play.

As it has been said many times, we are spiritual beings having a human experience. Each soul incarnate on this earth is playing a role, if you will, as a particular human being. If we embrace the notion that the world of the stage is a microcosm for the world at large, then suddenly things that have seemed esoteric, unattainable, and even un-attemptable, without extensive time spent in the lotus position on a mountain somewhere in Tibet, become straight forward and practicable.

Once the metaphor is truly embraced then there are clear things that you can do—not just think about, or ponder, but *do* immediately that will change your life in that instant. Whether playing a role on stage or playing the role in life, there are certain techniques, practices, and perspectives that, once understood, help us to play our role with focus, specificity, ease, authenticity, and clear purposeful intention.

ACTIVATING YOUR BRILLIANT TRUTH

Our unique creative genius and our purpose in the cosmic scheme of things is not a mystery or happenstance any more than an actor's performance in a play or a fabulously fluid improvisation is an accident. We are perfectly cast in our role in this life. We are here to be and do and have all that we desire. We were born with the genius to match our desire and the complete ability to bring it to fruition. Now we just have to ignite the fire of our brilliance and let it shine

I understand that igniting the fire of your brilliance probably sounds like a big deal and really difficult. It is and it isn't: it *is* a big deal and it *isn't* difficult at all. It's simple and quite natural. Just because we've forgotten the truth doesn't make it not true. And the truth is, you were born brilliant and you did it *on purpose*.

You have taken on this role on the great stage of life. You *chose* this. You created this reality you are currently engaged in and it's time now to start your training.

Think of this as the ultimate user's guide for a brilliant life. A metaphorical, metaphysical playbook for purposeful creation on the great stage of life. It's time to join the play, literally and figuratively. It requires a shift in thinking as well as simple, specific action steps to change habits and behaviors.

And more spoilers: these changes are easy to learn, sometimes hard to have faith in, often hard to remember to do, and they always hold the answer.

Once we combine these simple, basic elements together and set about practicing them on a daily basis, mindfully and intentionally, then life will become a festival of imagination, inspiration, and brilliant, almost magical, creative expression.

Are you ready?

CHAPTER 2

SETTING THE STAGE
FOR BRILLIANCE

"Through spontaneity we are re-formed into ourselves. ... Spontaneity is the moment of personal freedom when we are faced with reality, and see it, explore it and act accordingly. In this reality the bits and pieces of ourselves function as an organic whole. It is the time of discovery, of experiencing, of creative expression."

- **Viola Spolin**

MYTHS AND MISUNDERSTANDINGS

Let's start by clearing up a few things.

Our society is virtually flooded with myths. Myths are the stories we tell ourselves to explain what we don't understand. Cultural myths are those "answers" a society develops to address universal questions, concerns, or fears. Eventually, if enough of society is comforted or reinforced by the myth, it takes on the power of a truth.

Myth is defined by Merriam-Webster as:

- a popular belief or tradition that has grown up around something or someone. Especially: one embodying the ideals and institutions of a society or segment of society
- an unfounded or false notion.

Within the realm of creative genius, myths masquerading as truth and facts abound. They have become a narrative that explains why someone is valued less than someone else, or one group of humans is worth more than another. These stories we tell ourselves explain, enable, and disable each of us to varying degrees, preventing us from being the imaginative, creative geniuses we were born to be.

We've created huge myths and misunderstandings around a lot of human qualities and attributes. Words like imaginative, talented, creative, genius, innovative, and inventive are all labels to be aspired to in modern society. However, instead of seeing these attributes as inherent in our DNA, we view them as gifts given only to a select few. Yet I am absolutely certain, without ever having met you, that every single one of those seemingly exclusive monikers applies to you. Every single one of them reside in *your* DNA.

You are breathing; therefore you are imaginative, talented, creative, genius, innovative, and inventive. You are. No question. And so is everyone else.

I want you to repeat after me:

If it is true for any of us, it is possible for all of us, or else it isn't true at all.

STOP AND THINK

The first thing I ask any group of people I'm speaking to, whether the room is filled with CEO's, educators, entrepreneurs, artists, or students, is: "Raise your hand if you've ever had to stop and think."

So let's do that now. I'm asking you to raise your hand, please, if you've ever had to "stop and think" before you say something, decide to do something, or write something down.

Go ahead and literally raise your hand if you are alone. If you are reading this on an airplane or in a crowded room, just raise your hand in your mind, or perhaps just scratch your head.

Since I have been asking this question for over 35 years and I have never had anyone not raise their hand, I will proceed in the relative certainty that yours is in fact raised, at least in your mind. So, now that you have admitted to having to "stop and think" at some time in your life, let me share a little-known fact about that with you:

No, you didn't.

Humans think faster than we are able to perceive. In fact, we think so fast and so continuously that there is an ever-raging debate among experts on just how many thoughts we humans have in a day. The estimates vary greatly depending on the context, ranging from 6,400 measurable thoughts to 20,000 actionable thoughts to an average 60,000 recognizable thoughts to as many as 200,000 conscious and unconscious thoughts.

In any case, *it's a lot!* And the fact still remains that none of us who raised our hands had to "stop and think." We stopped, but not to think. So, what did we "stop" to do?

Of course, we all know the answer. We stopped to censor ourselves. We stopped to edit our thoughts. We stopped to consider, judge, and choose the "correct" thoughts, eliminating most of our 60,000 thoughts from becoming noticed as one of the conservative 6,000 or so that we might act upon, explore, build on, speak about, or write down.

The simple truth is that we humans have a plethora of thoughts every day, some we recognize and some we don't. We don't have to do anything special in order to have the thoughts. The *special* part comes with the recognition that we had a *particular* thought. The extra special part comes when the thought gets a chance to thrive—when it does not fall victim, for whatever reason, to the censor.

I've said it before and I'm sure I'll say it again: The problem is not a lack of thoughts. The problem is not a lack of creative thoughts. The problem is not a lack of brilliant thoughts.

You have a multitude of them!

The problem is that very few of us are very good at noticing them, allowing them, trusting them, expressing them, and acting on them.

THE CENSOR

When we are born, we arrive into this world without a censor. We express our spontaneous thoughts. If you doubt that, just hang out with a newborn who thinks it's time for dinner or a diaper change, and then watch them express that thought freely and at the top of their lungs.

Humans are born with both the gift of thoughts and with the gift of expressing them. The part we must be taught is to censor what we are thinking and to judge the usefulness or correctness of our thoughts. We are taught from birth to value particular thoughts more than others, to hide some thoughts, and to fear thinking others. By the time we graduate high school (let's be honest, usually by the time we graduate grade school), we are far better at judging, discarding, and ignoring most of our thoughts than we are at expressing them.

We're raised in an educational system that is totally based on assessments, calculations, and judgments of a particular kind of intelligence. Like the well-meaning monkeys, we are so enamored with the assessments of intelligence that we constantly revamp and enhance them, trying to find a more clever way to assess, calculate, and judge a student's level of intelligence. And, like the well-meaning monkeys, most people think that intelligence and creative genius are the same thing.

No, they are not.

Creative genius is something that each and every one of us is born with.

Despite the lack of comfort this fact may afford the well-meaning monkeys in the world, there is no way to codify or score it relative to the creative genius of others.

We each have our own gift of genius to bring to this planet. It is not a case of some people being gifted and others not. It's a case of some people finding their niche or their mode of expression and others not. After all these years, I am still regularly shocked and saddened at how many people think they are born with less brilliance than the gifted few. Somewhere along the line, they learned that their thoughts weren't the right kind of brilliant, and so they were worth less than someone else's thoughts.

Remember: it's not the brilliance that is lacking, it's the recognition, acceptance, expression, and utilization of that brilliance that we get hung up on. It's not hard for you to be brilliant. It can be challenging to express your brilliance and hard to get it acknowledged, but the brilliant part itself is a cinch.

You were born that way. You just forgot.

CONSIDER THE SIMPLE MATH

Conservatively speaking, let's say you have a possible 60,000 thoughts a day, and 20,000 of them are going to be recognizable or noticeable. You consider, and potentially act on, maybe 6,000 thoughts. Given those numbers, does it really seem that shocking that you might have at least one potentially brilliant thought out of the 6,000 each and every day?

What if that brilliant thought is one of the ones you discard, or worse yet, what if it's one of those that go unnoticed? We are taught to be mannered in our thinking and we usually become so measured, so restrained, that we end up intentionally limiting ourselves to repeating the same acceptable thoughts over and over again.

"We have approximately 60,000 thoughts in a day. Unfortunately, 95% of them are thoughts we had the day before."

- Deepak Chopra

OUR OWN PERSONAL MYTHS

We are, each of us, in a constant state of evaluation, judgment, and concern over our thoughts. Which thoughts will we share? Which thoughts are acceptable? Which thoughts are the right thoughts? Which thoughts should be put into words? And which thoughts should be acted upon?

The truly sad reality is that most of us make 99% of those decisions on autopilot. We all have "presets" built into our thinking based on either our interpretation of the feedback we got from our previously expressed ideas or our interpretation of the feedback we witnessed others receiving for theirs. So the presets that guide and limit our thinking were installed both directly through personal interaction or indirectly through observation from well before we had the thought we are currently judging.

Presets are tripwires. They are memories, moments in time, experiences that grow or become reinforced by our emotional reaction to them and our pursuit of survival and safety mentally, emotionally, and physically.

Presets develop into four possible results:

> **Preconceptions:** "I'm not good at that."
> **Expectations:** "There's no point. Why even try?"
> **Judgments:** "There must be something wrong with me."
> **Limiting Beliefs:** "Some people just aren't meant to win."

Preconceptions are thoughts we conceived prior to the moment at hand. Unfortunately, the more we say them or think them, the more they simply become habits. Once we've let a preconception become a habitual response, we are very unlikely to try to change it. It's become a given in our story.

Expectations can be dangerous little things. They are our internal predictions of the future. Our predictions become a self-fulfilling prophecy. When our predictions are negative, they destroy our opportunity for a positive outcome.

Judgments are the labels we place on ourselves and others. They are the identifying markers that develop both from and into our limiting beliefs. Though judgements can be both good and bad, they often limit our perspective.

Limiting Beliefs are negative presets that we see as truths. They literally set the limits or boundaries that we believe exist in our lives. Limiting beliefs are not conscious processes.

We practice our presets without even realizing it and get stuck in a loop. Our presets become habits and evolve into beliefs. We adopt those habitual beliefs into our lives and set about telling ourselves and each other what is true about us and the world. In effect, they are the prism through which we view ourselves and others. Our presets are so powerful they become our own personal myths. They become the myths we use to explain what's possible or isn't possible to be, do, or have.

THE MYTHOLOGY OF CREATIVITY

One of the saddest and most convoluted myths in our social consciousness is the myth of creativity. I can't tell you how many businesspeople, managers, and even teachers have told me "I'm not very creative" or they divide themselves and others into "non-creative" types vs "creative" types.

In literally every case, the problem has not been with the person's lack of creativity, but rather a confusion of the word "creative" with the word "artistic." Artistic refers to somebody in the arts—somebody who writes, draws, paints, sings, etc. Not everyone has a passion about, or affinity for, the arts. But everyone, *including you*, is most certainly creative.

If you've been a victim of this myth, it's not your fault. Even Webster lists the synonyms for artistic as: creative, imaginative, inventive, and expressive. Except you can be creative, imaginative, inventive, and expressive *and* not be given to a particular talent in, or passion for, the arts.

Scientists are creative, carpenters are creative, and parents are creative. You could very well be creative at collecting garbage, and I dare say that somebody truly has been. Whoever invented those claws on the sides of garbage trucks to pick up the cans was very creative! Just think of how many garbage collectors that creative person saved from rotator cuff surgery by stopping them from having to fling those cans. Have you watched those things? They are amazing, creative, and innovative, and we take them for granted instead of seeing them as brilliant.

THE CREATIVITY CRISIS

In 2010, IBM surveyed more than 1,500 chief executive officers from 60 countries and 33 industries. What they found was that chief executives believe that the most desired quality in order to succeed into the future was creativity. Creativity rated higher than rigor, management, discipline, integrity, or vision. And again in 2012, the CEO study results showed that leaders believe successful employees must be "collaborative, communicative, flexible, and creative." Also in 2012, an Adobe State of Create study showed that 75% of people feel increased pressure to be productive and only 25% feel that they are living up to their creative potential.

And thus, the so-called "Creativity Crisis" was born. The creativity crisis seems to be the primary reason for a flood of books and around eight billion TedTalks on creativity and the creative process. They are all there to combat the creativity crisis.

However, in case you haven't already guessed it, I'll just say it:

We don't have a creativity crisis.

We just *don't*.

Deciding that we have a creativity crisis or a shortage of creativity is like deciding that we have a shortage of breathing humans. Which, again, we just don't. We may not pay attention to their breathing, recognize their breathing as similar in significance to our own, consider their breathing as a valuable life-giving action, or rank their breathing as contributing anything to our world whatsoever. But the fact remains that they breathe. We breathe. Living human beings breathe and we create, too.

We do have a crisis, but it's a crisis of faith. It's a crisis of faith in ourselves and each other. It's a denial, or at least a doubt, that every human being we meet and encounter, no matter what their age, education, or circumstance, is a brilliant, creative genius in their own right. We lack faith in the inherent value of the ideas and inspirations of ourselves or those around us.

DEFINING CREATIVITY

For years, the same fears that have spawned the creativity crisis have bred widespread criticism of the educational system. Now clearly (as I've demonstrated in depth via metaphorical monkeys), I have some fairly harsh opinions about the educational system's effects on creativity and creative expression. And while I will agree that there are certainly a lot of issues with the systems inside of systems inside of systems that have been created by an untold number of well-meaning monkeys in the name of education, those systems are not the cause of the problem — they are a response or, as some would like to think, a solution.

But obviously, the problem is not solved, or we'd have creativity bursting out of every child in every classroom everywhere and every member of every workforce would feel empowered to express their creative genius. And *you* would feel excited and energized by your ideas and inspirations every day, following those that felt the most fun to fruition in playful abandon.

But the problem isn't solved because you cannot fix something that isn't broken.

Our creativity isn't broken, our *understanding* of it is.

Even the most brilliant, most well-meaning monkeys don't seem to realize that they are trying to codify a process that has no reason to exist, except to respond to the problem that they are helping to create. They are fundamentally misunderstanding and mischaracterizing creativity. To paraphrase our friend Mr. Einstein, they are trying to solve a problem at the same level of thinking that created it. Creativity is not the problem; judgment is the problem.

One of the most famous TedTalkers and authors on the subject of creativity is Sir Ken Robinson. I, like many millions of people, enjoy and respect the ideas of the late Sir Ken. He was a wonderful thought leader in the areas of education and creativity, their interconnectedness, and their diametric opposition.

When I began writing this book, I was looking for a definition of creativity that I could get behind. Naturally, I turned to Sir Ken. I was excited to learn that in 1999, Sir Ken headed a commission in the UK to develop a national strategy on creativity in education. One task of the commission was to come up with a definition for creativity. Thanks to Google, my expectant search only took a few minutes at most and there it was, Sir Ken and the commission's definition of creativity:

"The process of having original ideas that have value."

Really?! I can't even begin to tell you how saddened I was to see this absolutely topsy-turvy perspective on creativity out in the world! I know it's just nine little words. I know it seems harmless enough. But as much as I respect Sir Ken, I'm afraid that this definition is deeply flawed.

If I had asked a commission to deliberately come up with a definition of creativity that was inherently judgmental and stifling, I can't think of a better one than this. And within those nine words, two of them both encompass and perpetuate huge, destructive myths around creativity.

THE TROUBLING WORDS #1

I'm sure you can already guess at least one of the two words that I specifically take issue with. So let's begin with "value." It's not that I think creative ideas don't have value—they absolutely do. But the first question I would love to ask Sir Ken is: *"Of value, to whom?"*

I never thought I'd say this in a million years, but Sir Ken and his commission are sounding a little bit (OK, *a lot*) like the well-meaning monkeys. Remember, what the monkeys think is valuable and what the fish thinks is valuable are two completely different things!

We must allow, nurture, and respect the creative thoughts of everyone. If we judge those thoughts, which is what a word like value really implies, then somebody (and not the somebody having the thought, mind you) is deciding whether or not that thought is worthwhile. And if we judge an idea based on its believed potential outcome, before it has grown to its full potential, we are setting up an insurmountable standard for anyone who thinks at a different pace or in a different way than those doing the judging.

Imagine all the things that wouldn't be here if the people who had the idea stopped when another person judged it to have no value. Junius Morgan warned his son against investing in Thomas Edison's lightbulb. Even though he'd seen it in action, he thought electricity was a fad. Lucky for all of us, J.P. Morgan saw value where his father did not. Most importantly, Edison saw value in his own original ideas.

I could tell you the same kinds of stories about telephones and televisions. Even cars were thought of as expensive and impractical toys. People could not see the value, especially when these ideas were still in their fledgling states.

The idea that a creative thought must be judged to have value presupposes that there is some way to universally judge that value. And there is, but not what any well-meaning monkeys might believe it to be, because the validity of the creation doesn't rest in the mind of the critic, only in the heart of the creator.

Let me say that again:

The validity of the creation doesn't rest in the mind of the critic, only in the heart of the creator.

THE TROUBLING WORDS #2

The second word I have issues with is from the first part of the definition: *"the process of **having**."* What do they mean by "having?" We already know that having an idea is instantaneous; it's not a process. So the "process" they're referring to seems to be the process of establishing value. In that case, a more authentic definition would be: "The process of determining the value of an idea that you have had."

But that's the polar opposite of creativity!

We are far too used to judging the value of ideas before they get a chance to be developed, considered, or even recognized, let alone acted on in any way. We don't even need any well-meaning monkeys to do the judging. We judge our thoughts in our own heads before we ever express the idea and therefore it never gets the chance to come out and play.

So many versions of the creative process have an evaluation point in it somewhere that is almost always *way too early*! The truth is, many of the ideas one has in any creative process will evolve and evaluate themselves. That's what makes it a *process*.

Creativity is an evolutionary process. The lightbulb, the automobile, the internet, and every song you have ever heard were all ideas that evolved, and they were only allowed to do that because they were nurtured by their creator before they were judged. The judgment of an enlightened creation is far different than the judgment of the thought that could lead to said creation.

For instance, I like some of Bob Dylan's songs and don't care for others. But despite my opinions, he won a Nobel Prize in Literature. He is a poet laureate based on his body of work, not on the initial idea he had to write his first song or even his hundredth.

THE TROUBLING WORDS #3

That brings me to the third word I take umbrage with. I know, I know. I said there were only two, but this is not a word *in* the sentence. It's the word that is *missing from* the sentence. That word is "action."

The difference between imagination and creativity is that creativity requires action. Or as Sir Ken put it, "creativity requires outcomes," which would seem to nullify his own definition because again, creativity is active. Creativity is not having the idea, it is *using* the idea, developing it, building on it, adding it to more ideas, and finally creating something out of them.

Creativity is a process, but it's not the thought that is the process. It's what one does with the thought that is the process. Creation requires us to *do something*.

MY DEFINITION OF CREATIVITY

OK, here we go. I thought long and hard about this. After not finding a suitable definition of creativity as of the writing of this book, I came up with my own.

Creativity is the conscious and deliberate evolutionary process of developing a thought or thoughts in the imagination and then taking action on those thoughts in order to manifest change, alter perception, enhance understanding, or to bring into being something as yet unrealized in our awareness or physical reality.

I wish Sir Ken was still with us. I would love to discuss this further. But in lieu of that opportunity, let's chat.

THE MYTHOLOGY OF THE CREATIVE PROCESS

As soon as we got super serious about this supposed creativity crisis, we also got super serious about establishing the process for getting creative. Because, of course, that's what well-meaning monkeys do! In fact there is nothing more mythologized right now in the field of creativity than "The Creative Process." Just look at any 5 TedTalks on creativity and you'll find 5 slightly nuanced versions of The Creative Process.

Here's the simple truth about The Creative Process:

There isn't one.

Or should I say, there isn't *one*

The Creative Process doesn't exist. There are as many creative processes as there are individual human beings on this planet. It is not a step by step exactly ordered process that can be followed like a recipe with standardized results. But our systems and the well-meaning monkeys among us, really really *really* want a group answer. The truth is, there is no group answer because there is no group.

There is no one-size-fits-all answer because each of us has a singular, unique purpose and passion which we were born to discover and nurture and bring to light ourselves.

The key for each of us is to develop our own process that fits our unique creative genius and to honor and support the unique process of those around us.

I don't have to teach you to become creative, you *are*. You just need to become aware of how you create on the great stage of life.

So, what's the difference?

THE WRONG DEBATE

"Thoughts become things. Choose the good ones."

- Mike Dooley

I love this quote. So simple and yet so profound. And he's right, 100%. The most important word there is "choose." Choose your thoughts and then use them *intentionally*. That, my friends, is creating.

For forever, we have separated creativity and creation as though they are two different things. Because as limited as we might be in our own belief in our inherent creativity, we are far more limited in our ability to think of ourselves as creators. We have relegated the privilege of creating our lives and our experiences to forces outside ourselves. We abdicate the responsibility of, well, *us* to nature, happenstance, or The Universe.

Human beings in general seem to be prone to not taking responsibility for our own lives. We're really attracted to the idea that someone or something outside of us is going to either fix our problems or take the blame. But in acting as in life, there is no getting around the fact that we are 100% responsible for the character we are playing.

An actor, regardless of the work of the director, the other actors, the producer, or the playwright, is 100% responsible for their own performance. They are responding and making choices in the moment to what is happening throughout the course of the production. All the best laid plans of the other people involved don't remove the ultimate, full, and complete responsibility of the individual performance from the individual actor.

And that's us. We are that actor, creating our performance in this role.

We are all creating constantly. It's what we do. Our thoughts create actions. Our actions create outcomes. Actions cannot exist without thoughts.

As Lao Tzu said:

"Watch your thoughts, they become your words; watch your words, they become your actions; watch your actions, they become your habits; watch your habits, they become your character; watch your character, it becomes your destiny."

THINKING IS CREATING

Just as you are thinking thousands and thousands of thoughts each day, you are also creating. Constantly. 24/7, 365 days a year, you are creating. How do I know? Because of those 60,000 thoughts a day.

As Mary Morrisey often says:

*"Everything is created twice.
It had to be a thought before it could be a thing."*

Creativity is your ability to actively and consciously focus your thoughts. We are all creating because we are thinking. The trick is to learn to create intentionally, purposefully, with focus.

Creativity is a practice, not a trait.

This practice requires spontaneous thoughts, imagination, clear intention, and specific action.

We need spontaneous thoughts and imagination to be creative on this great stage of life. Before we embark on this creating odyssey, let me ask you: Have you got both of those?

Let's check.

CHAPTER 3
IMAGINATION AND SPONTANEITY

"Imagination is the beginning of creation. You imagine what you desire, you will what you imagine and at last you create what you will."

\-   George Bernard Shaw

THE MYTHOLOGY OF IMAGINATION

The imagination is so important and so fundamental that I feel like I should be writing it in all caps for emphasis — it's not just the imagination, it's THE IMAGINATION!!!

The imagination is the fundamental component of creativity. In fact, our imagination is the essential building block of our experience of life itself! OK, we'll get to that a little later, but the point is:

If anything is more misunderstood than creativity, it is…

THE IMAGINATION!!!

Most of us think that there is a possibility that our imagination might not work as well as someone else's. How many times have you heard or used the term "active imagination"? As in, *"Annie has a very active imagination."* It's generally used to refer to someone who expresses and follows their imagination openly. But this seemingly innocuous phrase is at the root of two common and highly damaging misconceptions about imagination. The first being that the phrase "active imagination" implies that there is such a thing as an "inactive imagination." But there is simply no such thing.

The second myth is that someone with an active imagination is a little "different" than the rest of the population, and not in a good way. When used as a derogatory term, active imagination is used as a synonym for fanciful or silly. It suggests that the person possessing the active imagination is less grounded in reality than those mythological figures with the inactive imaginations. The fastest way to clear up this set of myths is simply to substitute the word active with the word "allowed." The only real difference between what is considered an active or an inactive imagination is how much that imagination is allowed to be acknowledged and expressed.

We have so misunderstood the imagination, that we have conjured up the mythology that not everybody even has one. The following are direct quotes from actual prospective or beginning students of mine:

> *"Well, I don't really have much of an imagination."*

Or:

> *"I don't really have an imagination."*

And the ever popular:

> *"I have absolutely no imagination whatsoever."*

And in response, I can only share with you what I said to them at the time:

> ***"Oh, come on! Seriously?!"***

You have an imagination. Full stop. You have just as much of an imagination as everyone else does.

What is active or inactive, evident or not, is our willingness or ability to share our imagination with others or even with ourselves. What we view as a lack of imagination is actually our fear of judgment about the value of whatever we might imagine.

It's no wonder that many of us have decided we don't have one, or ours doesn't work, because our imagination has gotten a really bad rap. It's become responsible for all things silly, pointless, unfounded, inconvenient, and wrong.

Even those of us who have maintained a belief in our imagination have had to weather the constant dismissal of imagination as something of no value. How often have you heard in response to an idea or feeling that you've expressed: "Oh, that's just your imagination." How many times has that been said to you, have you said it to someone else, or have you said it to yourself? Whatever the number of times, *it's too many*.

You are hereby invited to change that practice and welcome your imagination to come out and play. And don't worry, it will. Because regardless of how you may feel about using it, the fact remains that you have a beautiful, fully-fledged, profoundly able imagination. It is a basic, hard-wired human trait. It works on both the conscious and subconscious levels and it is constantly active. It is far more powerful than any other one of our mental processes or faculties and it's time for us to recognize that and start consciously utilizing it.

"Imagination is more important than knowledge. Knowledge is limited. Imagination encircles the world."

- Albert Einstein

I THINK, THEREFORE I AM IMAGINING

Imagination is thought, and therefore, as we know, it is happening all the time, effortlessly, and much more than we realize. Imagination is actually our default way of thinking.

If your imagination seems AWOL, it's not because it is actually missing—it's just atrophied. Or, more accurately, your awareness of it and your interaction with it has atrophied. It's the conscious and deliberate use of your imagination that is not happening. Your imagination is there, you use it constantly to visualize, to tell stories, to develop ideas, and to understand what you perceive. We just need to awaken your awareness and then get that imagination exercised, and nurtured.

You may not be practiced at consciously and deliberately recognizing and expressing what is in that imagination. You may not believe that your imaginings are worthwhile. You may not utilize your imagination intentionally, but you can, and you will.

THE POWER OF IMAGINATION

According to Merriam-Webster, the definition of imagination is:

- The act or power of forming a mental image of something not present to the senses or never before wholly perceived in reality.

Imagination is also our most important and powerful thought process.

We have others, such as perception, reason, knowledge, memory, and analysis. Arguably, all of them require imagination in order to be productive or creative. Without imagination, we have no evolution of what is to what might be. I mean, come on! Even Mr. Webster calls it a power!

Another way that Webster defines imagination is "a creation of the mind." I love that. A creation of the mind — is there any other kind? Imagination is the foundation of creativity, for *all* that we create.

> *"If you can imagine it, you can achieve it.*
> *If you can dream it, you can become it."*

> - William Arthur Ward

Everything around you, all the objects that you use, all the things that you eat, everything that you wear, the computer or book you are reading this on right now, were all thoughts before they became physical reality. They were imagined first. They began in the realm of infinite possibility, which is accessed through your imagination, and then they became part of this reality, this great world stage where we currently play.

IMAGINATION IS THE PLAYGROUND OF THE SOUL

Imagination is a very powerful tool. It is the bridge between the soul and the mind. As I have said, it is the way in which we bring what might be into what is. It is with our imagination that we understand possibility and envision what we desire. It is with our imagination that we solve problems, understand ourselves and each other, and bring our intuition and divine inspiration into fruition. Like creativity, imagination is both innate and is something that can get stronger and more fluid with practice.

Your imagination is also singular to you. It is one of the primary factors that makes your creative genius unique. It is your metaphysical watermark, as individual as a fingerprint. It is your unique access point to the wonders of the Universe. This individual creative fingerprint is not something to judge, but something to celebrate and use!

HAVING SOUL

When an actor's performance is said to "have no soul," it is when the performance seems mechanical or matter-of-fact rather than being connected to the very soul of the actor. What I tell my actors in a case like this, is that I don't believe them because their imagination is not alive in the present moment. They are not responding within the context of what is actually happening in this moment. They are basing their reactions and choices on the experiences of the past and the expectation of what they assume others will do and say.

"In acting as in life." When the soul (the imagination) is connected and responding in the present moment, that is the moment of spontaneous brilliance. In case you haven't noticed, "spontaneous" is the operative word here.

SPONTANEITY DEFINED

In order to express your genius, you must nurture and develop *your* thoughts and ideas. In order to develop a thought, you must first recognize that you have it. In order to act on it, you have to notice that it's there and then allow it to see the light of day. That requires getting in touch with the essential element that is often left out of, or at the very least significantly downplayed, in most iterations of the supposed creative process: imagination's dearest buddy, spontaneity.

Dictionary.com's definition of spontaneity is:

- Resulting from a natural impulse or tendency; without effort or premeditation; natural and unconstrained; unplanned.

In the words of Lucy Van Pelt (of Charlie Brown fame):

"THAT'S IT!!!"

That's the point. Your spontaneous, unvarnished thoughts — that's where the magic is. Not that every thought is magic, but if you don't explore your thoughts, trust your thoughts, and express your thoughts, then how will you ever find the magical, brilliant ones?

The value of the spontaneous thought simply can't be overstated. That is where the brilliance lies, in the momentary impulse, inspiration, and intuition, that most of us typically discount or spring past. That's where genius is hiding, just waiting for you to grab hold of it.

We so undervalue the spontaneous thought that we don't just not nurture it, but we purposefully blow it off. Ignoring that spontaneous thought, that spontaneous impulse, is the stifling structure at the heart of our education system. We are taught to be mannered in our thinking and usually become so measured and restrained that we end up intentionally limiting ourselves to repeating the same thoughts over and over again. After all, spontaneity is inconvenient; we have important things to do. Anyone who has managed to maintain or retain their spontaneity throughout their education and into adulthood is probably viewed as disruptive. And that is terribly unfortunate because actually capturing the spontaneous thought is one of the great secrets to a truly brilliant life.

Spontaneity cannot be overvalued. Our ability to deal with it as such is exactly the same as our ability to be present in the moment. This world is spontaneous! We do not know what is around the next corner. No matter how much we plan, we cannot control what happens next. All we can do is learn to roll with it and add to it and that requires our aware engagement with our thoughts.

If we want to seek our own, personal brilliance, we have to learn a different way of behaving so that we can readily recognize and access our spontaneous thoughts. Spontaneity requires a natural, unconstrained, and unplanned process that is both joyful and fearless — or at least not fearful.

"How do we do that?" you may ask. At this stage of the game, the irony is that to regain spontaneity, we have to relearn it. We have to relearn how to play. And once we relearn it, we can restore that natural part of our psyche to the state of open wonder and unconstrained thought and allow ourselves to play in the field of unlimited possibilities. We do that by raising our awareness, building our connection to our imagination, and letting go of expectations so that we can notice the beautiful,

unexpected connections that our imagination will spontaneously make for us.

RELEARNING HOW TO PLAY

If I ask an adult to pretend, to imagine for a moment that they are a nurse, they smile, nod, and consider that idea. They might even visualize themselves in a nurse's uniform, doing nurse things. If I try to encourage them to go with it and actually stand up and physically "act out" being a nurse, they'll likely scowl at me and think I'm crazy for being so ridiculous as to ask them to do such a thing in the first place. After all, they are not a nurse; they are a political scientist, and a really smart, really cool person! What's wrong with me?!

However, if I ask a child to pretend that they are a nurse, they get up and start doing nurse things. They are immediately engaged in the enjoyment of doing. When they engage in doing, they are immediately enjoying.

As powerful as thought is, that is not what we came here to do. We came here to *play the role*! We came here to do stuff, not just think about stuff or watch other people do stuff!

The reason that the adults do it in their heads and the kids actually do it is not because the adults don't understand how to play, how to pretend, and how to act it out. It's because they no longer believe that is an acceptable way to behave. It's not cool. It's not allowed.

SPONTANEOUS CREATURES

We are all born spontaneous creatures. We are impulsive, often irrational, and act on our instincts. And then what happens? Well basically, we learn not to let ourselves do that. There is a time and a place for standing on a chair and screaming, "I know! I know!!!" — which is apparently not when the teacher asks who knows the answer to the question written on the board in your 3rd grade class, as Ahmed did. Everyone else in the class who didn't stand on their chair and scream had learned that already. Whether or not a chair-stand screech is useful, helpful, or even accurate is irrelevant. It is not the accepted behavior in that circumstance, and so it is wrong. And Ahmed is in trouble. Again.

Now, it's possible that Ahmed could innately know more about the answer to the question than the teacher does. Ahmed could be a unique creative genius with the ability to answer this question, and many others, on this topic in ways that no one has ever quite thought of before, the realization of which could lead the human race to untold technological discoveries.

However, since Ahmed is likely a metaphorical fish in a room full of monkeys, we clearly have a problem. If he buys into the idea that it's best to behave like a monkey, we may never see another spontaneous expression of his unique creative genius ever again.

But, if we are very lucky, Ahmed could have a teacher (perhaps a giraffe) who expects that each of her students possesses a unique creative genius and therefore understands that an outburst like Ahmed's is something to be channeled and nurtured rather than cut off or punished.

And if this teacher has the tools to help Ahmed express his answer and build upon it, and collaborate with others to develop it, they can cultivate Ahmed's enthusiasm into a lifelong respect for his own ideas and the ideas of others.

TAKING THE LEAP

I began teaching acting and improv in New York in 1986. My first several years as a teacher were in a conservatory. The students and the instructors were focused on developing their craft, deepening their understanding, and growing as creative artists and human beings. I was in a kind of naive teaching bliss. But in 1989, I was in for a rude awakening. That was the first time I had an appointment at a regular liberal arts university. I had attended and even graduated with honors from a university, once upon a time. I knew what it was like. But in my naïve artist/young acting teacher bliss, I had somehow managed to forget.

I was shocked to realize that the students were more interested in how to get a certain grade than in how to explore, play, examine, learn, develop, and grow. I had my first taste of the fact that the adults I was teaching had forgotten how to play. They didn't want to take chances. They didn't want to speak up and speak out. They didn't want to explore their ideas — they wanted to parrot mine. Because what they really, really wanted was the grade. They had given up the spontaneous thought for the guaranteed grade. They'd had the joy of learning and the magic of spontaneous exploration educated right out of them.

These students, in both undergraduate and graduate performance programs, were not developing how to be the best "them" they could be. They did not bring offers of new ideas to class and build on the concepts they learned to make them their own. They did not imagine that they were just as much their own teacher as I was. They were completely consumed by the system, seeking the approval of the teacher, the grader, the department chair, the thesis committee, their peers, their audiences... but they were not following their soul, listening to their own inner genius, and, worst of all, they were not having any fun.

These grownups had not only forgotten how to play, they were actually *afraid* to play. They did not see even creative endeavors as fields of infinite possibilities. They saw class, rehearsal, and performance as a zero-sum game, where one could succeed or fail based on a grade.

When I told them: *"You have an A."*

When I told them: *"The only way you can lose that A is if you do not try."*

When I told them: *"Succeeding at what you try is not a factor."*

When I told them: *"Taking action, trying, giving it a shot, playing, being willing to take a chance – that is what I am looking for."*

They blinked and repeated: *"Yeah... but how do I get an A?"*

The tape was stuck.

I watched repeatedly as my, *"You already have your A, let's just explore, experience, and discover, the A will still be there,"* method caused huge amounts of anxiety in otherwise perfectly healthy, reasonable, intelligent, capable adults.

That was really the beginning. I created a course called "Imagination and Spontaneity." It was an improvisational exploration of the imagination and recognizing the spontaneous impulse. The class was equal parts improvisation technique and exploration, imagination/spontaneity exercises (often created spontaneously by me during a given class, even though I didn't tell the students that), as well as philosophy, human behavior, movement, voice improv, sound improv, and play, play, play, and more *play*.

I taught the class solely for the purpose of reconnecting adult students to the spontaneous thought. Brave souls in colleges and universities were willing to take the course, and I found that remarkably, in a class named "Imagination and Spontaneity," they were more willing to believe in my non-grading grading system.

Interestingly, the students who wanted to take the class began to come from all different disciplines and walks of life. In fact, all these years into it, I would have to say that, of the hundreds and hundreds of students that have taken such a class of mine, perhaps only a quarter of them were on a trajectory to become a performing artist of any kind. I have been stunned, more than once, at the diversity of majors in a single class. For example, in addition to several theater majors, and a few communications majors, one single class also had students with majors in: geoscience, engineering, anthropology, political science, education, computer science, radiology, physics, nursing, history, music, criminal justice, creative writing, environmental science, linguistics, and finance.

Whatever their interests, whatever their talent, whatever their life choices to that point, it made no difference. They walked in with no idea what they were getting themselves into and walked out ten times braver, ten times more aware, ten times more playful, and ten times more certain that they were capable of more imagination, creativity, and brilliance than they ever imagined.

Organically, all of my teaching became about asking people to take a leap of faith. I asked them to try. I asked them to trust. I asked them to be willing to believe that if they would do something, *anything*, that they would open themselves up to the possibility of brilliance. Through leaping, re-leaping, and re-re-leaping, the whole process got less and less scary. As the number of leaps grew, so did the statistical possibility that what sprang from them would be truly brilliant.

Quite often over the years, I have found it necessary to shout to my students or the professional actors in one of my productions, *"Lighten up, people! There is a reason why they call it a play! This is supposed to be fun!"* So consider this my shoutout to you:

Lighten up! This is supposed to be fun!

Now, if all it took to help you have fun was to tell you to have fun, this book would be a lot shorter.

Games are always a lot more fun to play once we understand the rules. We like to play games that challenge us, but we also like to know that we have a way to transcend that challenge. We continue playing games that we feel like we are getting better at, because succeeding is fun. The more skill we have at a game, the more confident we feel and the more fun we have playing it. People tend to improve at games they like and like games they are good at playing — it's a loop.

It's time to leap.

CHAPTER 4
AN IMPROVISATIONAL LIFE

"Good improvisers seem telepathic; everything looks pre-arranged; This is because they accept all offers made— which is something no 'normal' person would do."

\- **Keith Johnstone**

THIS MYTH IS NOT A METAPHOR

By now, we all know I love a good metaphor. Goodness knows, I will likely be referring to them many more times in the course of this book, but not at the moment. "Life is an improvisation" is not a metaphor. It is a factual, literal statement. And please note, I'm not saying that it could be, or that some people live that way, or that some moments are that. Life *is* that. All of it. That's all there is.

Life is an improvisation, by definition — literally.

Merriam-Webster:

Improvise:

- To speak, act or perform without preparation.
- To make or create (something) by using whatever is available.

Dictionary.com:

Improvise:

- To speak or act on the spur of the moment.
- To make, provide, or arrange from whatever materials are readily available.
- To compose, utter, deliver, execute, or arrange anything without previous preparation.

See what I mean? You are, by definition, improvising constantly. And now you are about to get more conscious of it and infinitely more aware of how to do it.

The first step to living a spontaneously brilliant, creative life is to step into—or should I say *leap* into—the improvisation willingly and purposefully. It's easy because, just like thinking and imagining, you already do it constantly.

AN IMPROVISATIONAL LIFE IN A SPONTANEOUS WORLD

When we say life is an improvisation, it is just another way of saying we live in a spontaneous world. When sages, teachers, and thought leaders are trying to educate us to be in the moment, to be present, to be mindful, to be in the now, they are asking us to be in flow with the spontaneity of the Universe in which we live.

Improvisation is really nothing more and nothing less than learned present moment thinking.

Improvisation, and therefore life, is about learning to be spontaneous on purpose. Learning the fundamentals of improvisation is learning to share the spontaneous thoughts that arise and deal with the spontaneous events that occur, all with the same faith, confidence, fluidity, and assurance that you do in a "planned" moment. It's the ultimate guide to rolling with the flow and making the most out of every moment.

SIMPLE VS EASY

The truth is that improvisation is ridiculously simple, even if it isn't always easy. It takes practice and it involves changing habits over time, but the basic principles of improvisation are not only very simple and profound, you are *already* doing these things every minute of every day. The only difference between how you do them *now* and how you will do them *from now on* is that you will do them mindfully and intentionally.

So, we're going to bust the myth that improv is hard. Though the concept strikes terror into the hearts of many, it is not really a fear of improvisation — it is actually fear of the unknown, the unexpected, of being out of control, of looking foolish, and of failing. Which are exactly the same fears we all have in life.

The irony of it all is that once you learn the fundamentals of improvisation and apply and practice them in your life, you will be far less likely to be afraid because you will be in a constant state of preparedness for the beautiful unexpected that is most assuredly coming your way.

THE MOST IMPORTANT THING YOU WILL EVER LEARN

In improv as in life, everything you think, do, and say is one of these three things:

Offering
Accepting
Blocking

In every improvisation, everything that a player does or says boils down to one of these three things, therefore in life the same is true. Everything you say or do or even think, as well as everything you encounter and everything you experience, is one of those same three things: The making of an **Offer,** the **Accepting** of an offer**,** or the **Blocking** of an offer**.**

It's not only ridiculously simple, but also so profound that nearly every philosophical and spiritual truism since the dawn of humankind can be reduced to some aspect of these concepts.

- **When we offer, we create.**
- **When we accept, we collaborate with compassion.**
- **When we block, we are in fear.**

So what should we do?

Well, in improv as in life we should offer, we should accept, and we should not block.

Did I mention it was simple?

DEFINING THE BASICS

Offering Defined:

> **In improvisation:** *Anything an actor does or says that adds to the situation*

> **In life:** *Anything you contribute in thought, word, or deed to any and all situations*

Offering is the fundamental component of creation. In order to create, grow, move, or build, we must offer.

Offers are powerful and very, very easy to make. For example, reading this right now is an offer, one that you are making to yourself. Once you acknowledge that it is an offer, then that requires you to build on it. Acknowledging offers is accepting responsibility. Every offer made is pure potential creativity, so is every offer that comes to you, if you choose to accept it and build on it. See how this works?

Accepting Defined:

In improvisation: *Acknowledging, incorporating, or including what the other actor has offered*

In life: *Acknowledging, incorporating, or including everything that comes into our experience in any relationship, situation, or interaction as an offer that is to be built upon*

Accepting allows us, and even **requires** us, to see everything that comes into our experience as an offer. By accepting, you are allowing the offer to develop or to further the situation. In essence, accepting says "I hear you, I see you" to a person, a behavior, an event, or an idea and incorporating it into the situation — as opposed to ignoring it or contradicting it, which would be blocking.

Blocking Defined:

In improvisation: *Directly contradicting or resisting any offer, stopping the action from developing*

In life: *Directly contradicting or resisting any offer or idea, stopping the situation from developing. Giving no validity, power, understanding, or consideration to the offer*

Thanks to our presets (preconceptions, judgments, expectations, and limiting beliefs), most of us are unconscious habitual blockers. We don't think of it as bad; we think of it as protection, independence, standing up for ourselves, being assertive, or being careful. We block out of fear, we block out of convenience, we block out of lack of understanding, we block to feel in control, and we block to feel comfortable. Blocking is the opposite of creativity. You cannot be creative and block at the same time.

THE KEY

For an improvisation to go well—which means for *life* to go well—there must be a constant series of offering and accepting. It's like a tennis match: back and forth. I offer, you accept. You offer, I accept. I offer… and so on. Anytime things are not flowing, there is a block.

So, just as in any improvisation, in your life your goal in every moment is to either make an offer and/or accept an offer and not to block.

It's that simple!

So here's the key to a conscious improvisational life.

Repeat after me:

Accept everything as an offer.
When in doubt, offer!
If in doubt, you are probably blocking.

THE MAGIC OF ACCEPTING

Accepting, at its essence, is the practice of saying "yes" to life. Accepting is acknowledging everything as an offer or "gift" that brings with it possibilities, lessons, and opportunities.

And there you have it. That's how it's done. You accept all offers made.

Every offer has the ability to be an amazing opportunity if you make it one. Now, I'm not suggesting that every offer is a gem — some offers are lazy, some offers are blocks disguised as an offer, and some offers are selfish. But prejudging an offer, in itself, is a block.

If you begin living an improvisational life, on purpose, by practicing the acceptance of every offer made to you, you will find that accepting becomes your natural response.

It's about establishing a practice of noticing what you have been given and accepting it as an offer. It's not about trying to choose between offers or judging whether an offer is good enough. If offers are neither good nor bad, but just *are*, then we can start to look upon it as our responsibility to offer back without being pulled into a judgment cycle.

If we can learn to embrace the cycle of accepting every offer and then offering something back that will build upon that offer, we will be in a constant state of ease and grace.

ACCEPTING A NEGATIVE

It is also important to note that, in improv and in life, just as an offer is not always nice or kind, accepting does not necessarily have to be nice or kind. Accepting also does not mean that you are agreeing with the offer. Agreeing and accepting are not the same thing. This is, again, why I will sometimes use the word "acknowledging" interchangeably with accepting. You are acknowledging the offer and accepting it as a part of reality.

Accepting does not mean surrender. It does not mean you take anything that someone dishes out and accept it as right or good. It means you notice what is happening. You notice the offers of others, conscious and unconscious, and you treat them as offers. You accept them into the moment, and you build on them.

Accepting means acknowledging the contribution — the offer you make in return is up to you.

REQUIRED SPONTANEITY

When we eliminate blocking, we have spontaneity. If we are not censoring and judging, which is the root of blocking, then we are spontaneous in our responses. The way to make ourselves more spontaneous is to require ourselves to offer and accept. One of the great things about offering and accepting is that, when we become practiced in them, we can override our presets.

Blocking is almost always about fear. I would even go so far as to say that, other than the occasional accidental block, blocking is *always* about fear. Blocking is resistance. Resistance is our response to fear.

Frightened improvisers (on stage and in life) stop things from moving forward by not accepting. Frightened improvisers block unconsciously and habitually to save themselves from fear and give themselves the illusion of control. Frightened improvisers cause their own boredom by not making deliberate offers to their own life.

The way to break through our knee-jerk protective reactions is to play the game of offering and interrupt the natural impulse to block.

THE PRACTICE OF "YES, AND…"

The most straightforward way to practice accepting all offers is to simply follow the pattern of the popular improv game, "Yes, and…" This game is set up as a simple framework to teach accepting and offering. You start with accepting as a matter of course and then immediately follow with an offer. If you start with "yes," you are by necessity accepting and then the "and" sets you up to return an offer. "Yes, and…" deflects blocks, or, in essence, incorporates them as if they were an offer.

In an improv class, it's a game used to ingrain a fundamental pattern of accepting and offering. Students literally say, "Yes, and…" out loud every time. It's a stilted process at first, but it's actually an easy habit to get used to. Obviously in life, you don't have to actually say "Yes, and…" out loud each time someone speaks. But in your head, it's an important pattern to acknowledge in order to gain consciousness of how often you are habitually blocking.

It's so wonderfully simple that it has now become the response that you hear the minute you mention improvisation as a concept or a teaching tool in any environment. This phrase has come to be recognized as a foundational philosophy rather than a simple tool.

EXAMPLES OF "YES, AND…"

WILL: Nico! Wow! You look amazing today! [OFFER]

NICO: Yes, and it's about time you noticed! I've been trying to get your attention for weeks! [YES, AND…]

Or:

WILL: Nico! Wow! You look amazing today! [OFFER]

NICO: Yes, and don't touch me, this dress costs more than you make in a year. [YES, AND…]

Or:

WILL: Nico! Wow! You look amazing today! [OFFER]

NICO: Yes, and it's all thanks to my new trainer, Klaus. [YES, AND…]

STOPPING THE FLOW

Improvisation is easy and engaging when a series of offers are being made and accepted by both parties. Remember: we are passing the ball back and forth. It's not enough just to catch the ball. If you hold onto it and don't send it back, the game is over.

Accepting without making an offer is blocking and will stop the flow.

Let me demonstrate.

ACCEPTING WITHOUT AN OFFER

WILL: Nico! Wow! You look amazing today! [OFFER]

NICO: Thank you. [ACCEPTED, NO OFFER]

(Result: Crickets and discomfort for Will.)

Or:

WILL: Nico! Wow! You look amazing today! [OFFER]

NICO: No, I don't. [BLOCKING, NO OFFER]

(Result: **Thud.**)

In both cases, no offer was made by Nico.

BLOCKING WITH AN OFFER

There are instances where blocking can include an offer. In this instance, at the very least, Will has something to build on.

WILL: Nico! Wow! You look amazing today! [OFFER]

NICO: No, I don't. [BLOCK] *But you do.* [OFFER]

Now the field is open for Will to respond. They have something to build on, and this conversation/improvisation could go in a million different ways from here depending on the level of accepting and offering that Will does in this moment.

In this case, their offer was blocked and then an offer was made, so Will has to choose between which they will deal with, the block or the offer.

A FEW POSSIBLE WILL RESPONSES

WILL: You think so? I was going for a new look today! Thanks for noticing! [IGNORING THE BLOCK, ACCEPTING THE OFFER, AND MAKING ANOTHER OFFER]

—

WILL: Well, thank you. But I really mean it. You do look amazing. [ACCEPTING THE OFFER, ACKNOWLEDGING THE BLOCK, AND REPEATING THE SAME OFFER]

In essence, this is not making an offer. Now we are in the land of "Nuh-uh!" and "Yeah, huh!" Or my personal favorite, "Do not!" and "Do, too!" This is a boring, frustrating, dead-end symphony of blocking caused by attachment to what came before.

BLOCKING DOES NOT HAVE TO BE ANTAGONISTIC

Remember: blocking is anything that contradicts, negates, or resists the value of the offer. It can be hostile, but it is not hostile by definition. Passive blocking sneaks up on us and we may not even recognize it as blocking because we expect blocking to feel aggressive. Our interaction tends to falter, and we don't know how to respond. In reality, passive blocking can be some of the most debilitating because we rarely manage to not take it personally.

IT'S A SPONTANEOUS WORLD

In improv as in life, don't get attached to the outcome.

We cannot control the outcome of an improv, just as we can't really control the outcome of the situations in our lives. We can and should set goals, which is to say we can and should set our *intentions*. What hinders us is when we set our *expectations* and get tied to the outcome.

As Marci Schimoff sums it up:

> *"Intention, Attention, No Tension."*

Now, of course we make plans in our lives. Life is a journey. On any journey, we have to plan where we intend to go in order to get there. But often when we plan, we set up expectations alongside our intentions. And if we get tied to the expectation of the outcome, then we end up blocking anything that does not fit that expectation. When we try to force an outcome by only offering and accepting those things that we thought of ahead of time, we limit our possibilities and create a boring improv — which, as we know, creates a boring life.

When we try to force others to make the choices we want them to make, it hinders our ability to accept what is really being offered to us and blocks both the offer we were given and any future offer we could receive, which is a recipe for frustration.

> *"To succeed, planning alone is insufficient.*
> *One must improvise as well."*

> - Isaac Asimov

It's tricky, I know. We get a plan, we set our intention, we release our attachment to the expected outcome, and we set about offering and accepting our way to our intended destination. It's a balancing act.

Imagine getting into our car to go somewhere. Most of us do this every day. We have a plan for our journey, how to get from point A to B. So we get into the car, start the car, plug the destination into our GPS, pull out of the driveway (all of these things are offers, by the way), and start toward our destination. But along the way, those spontaneous, unplanned things are bound to happen.

For instance, we could encounter a family of ducks in the middle of the road. The average driver doesn't plan for

AN IMPROVISATIONAL LIFE

ducks, just like ducks don't plan for traffic. But here's a new, spontaneous offer from, of all things, ducks! And that does not coincide with the plan.

But plan or not, now we have a veritable plethora of choices for how we accept the offer of the ducks, block the offer of the ducks, or make an offer to the ducks.

If we recognize the ducks as an offer (which they are), then we've got this. If we see the ducks as a block, well, it's not going to be nearly as much fun.

Blocking ducks are an annoying traffic issue, literally blocking our path on the way to our planned destination. Offering ducks, however, are a spontaneous interruption. Perhaps they walked into the road to remind us to stop and smell the roses, whether those roses are flipping to a different radio station, enjoying a conversation with our driving companion, or simply watching little duck feet slap against the asphalt.

The first offer to the ducks was stopping the car, so now what? What would your next offer be? You could honk, complain, inch the car forward to try and move the ducks along faster (this never works), or perhaps you could be so overwhelmed with concern for the ducks' welfare that you jump out of the car to ensure they safely cross the road.

It's up to you.

ACCEPTING AS A GRATITUDE PRACTICE

Once we embrace the cycle of offering and accepting, we can begin to recognize that every occurrence in our life is

81

an offer that is happening *for* us, not *to* us. Whether we view the ducks as an offer or not, they just intrinsically are. And, whether we recognize it or not, every offer is a gift.

We are taught from an early age that, when we receive a gift, we should say "thank you." We think of that as gratitude. But gratitude is more than just a verbal expression, it is a feeling that comes from within our souls.

Now that might strike you as a bit overstated, but it's not. It's just that we've gotten used to taking gratitude for granted. Truly, the more we engage in connecting with the soulful expression of gratitude, the more profound an experience just being *in* gratitude can be.

But we need to practice giving gratitude our full attention. Even for just a second. Even in the most trivial of circumstances. Embracing the cycle of offering and accepting as one of gift giving and receiving is like taking the game of "Yes, and…" and turning it into a game of "Yes, thank you, and…" In this game, the gratitude is automatic, just like the "yes." Most importantly, they both come before the "and…" In other words, the offer that you make is irrespective of the gratitude deserved by the offer that you received, whatever it may be.

Even ducks.

CHILDLIKE WONDER

The wonder that we marvel at in children is the complete acceptance and awareness of this world as spontaneous. The phrase "childlike wonder" is often used by adults to describe, with admiration or even envy, a child's ability to notice and accept all the offers coming to them.

When we say that about an adult, it is usually indicative of someone we find to be an out of the box thinker, an authentic, spontaneous, and often quite happy person inspired by the simple things in life. We marvel at or judge their awareness of the spontaneous world because we've had that awareness trained out of us. We have been taught, we come to believe, and we teach our children that a world we are in control of is better, and we gain that control through making plans.

But, au contraire, plans are the things we make that life interrupts.

As Allen Saunders said:

> **"Life is what happens to us while**
> **we are making other plans"***

> *(*I know, John Lennon quoted it in a song,*
> *but Allen Saunders is who he was quoting.)*

Every moment is an amalgam of spontaneous events, mashed up with the plans and expectations we bring to that moment. There are two kinds of spontaneous events: those you embrace (accept) and those you resist (block). Thus, if we learn to respond in the moment to the offers before us, keeping mindful of our plans, hopes, and dreams, we can successfully incorporate the planned with the improvised in order to create a beautiful, rich experience.

Plans are not bad. Plans can be necessary. Plans act as a springboard, a guide, and an inspiration. But plans need to be based on big goals and big objectives, not the minute details of the outcome. If you get hung up in the minutia, you will block offers.

You can only control *your own* offers. Trying to control someone else's offer is actually blocking. Remember, offers are not just things that others do or say — every being, place, thing, and event that comes into your life is an offer.

It's all about accepting what comes next.

MY TEACHING TODDLER

When I was teaching in the early 90's in the professional actor training program at the University of Utah, I gave birth to my oldest daughter, Shelly. Her father and I made a point of always having her with one of us. So when he was in classes, I would have her with me.

In improv classes, I would put her into a walker and let her wander the huge, gymnasium-sized room we used for a classroom. I would instruct my students that, if a baby wandered into their improv, they had to acknowledge her and make her a part of what they were doing. Likewise, if she left, they had to deal with that as well.

It became an unanticipated, wonderful tool for teaching my students to accept every event as an offer and build on it, regardless of whether it fit the "plan" or not.

Of course, the first time a baby scooted her way into the middle of their improvisation, their first instinct was to want to normalize it, explain it, or make it fit, which is just a version of blocking. They were especially prone to blocking the baby showing up if they thought their improv was going well. In fact, the level of blocking the students did when she showed up was in direct inverse proportion to the degree to which they perceived their improvisation to be successful prior to her arrival.

The more attached they were to what was happening, the more they blocked the idea of it changing. Their willingness to have a truly spontaneous response had evaporated as an unconscious plan had started to evolve. Often our plans start to develop as the ego gets involved and we get attached to the outcome.

And so it is in life.

It happens to all of us, almost constantly. We don't even realize that we are planning, let alone that we are growing attached to our expected outcomes. The more attached we are to the story, the plan, or the anticipated outcome, the more we unconsciously block the offers coming to us.

IMPROV WITH EYES OPEN

When a small child tries to block out what they do not want or like, they close their eyes, stick their fingers in their ears, and go, "Lalala lala… I can't hear you!" The child does it overtly. *They* know they are doing it and *we* know they are doing it.

As we become older (and supposedly more mature), we pride ourselves on developing subtle, covert methods of filtering out that which we don't want. We never even realize that we are training ourselves to block our attention to the present moment, limiting our connection to the offers being made by everything and everyone around us. We consider maturity being able to focus our attention, and it is. But there is a difference between focusing our attention and limiting our attention.

The real task is to pay attention and really listen without agenda or preconceived notions, to the world around us. This is not just limited to our relationships with humans — if you really listen to animals, or the environment, or your car, they will tell you a great deal. It's about discovering what is there, rather than deciding it or proving a preconceived notion.

If you aren't listening and paying attention in each moment, you are not noticing, let alone accepting, the offers coming to you. That means any offers you are making are being made from your ego and "the plan." They are coming from expectation and from a place of controlling, not from a place of accepting.

Remember that improvisation is learned, present moment thinking. You can't plan an improv. You must be present to discover what is happening moment by moment, instant by instant, offer by offer.

An important part of being a conscious creator is to see literally everything as an offer. If you are seeing everything as a gift for exploration, collaboration, or even introspection on your part, then you are well on your way to the graceful process of conscious creation.

As I said, the concepts are simple, though practicing them is not always easy. The tricky part is getting familiar with when you are offering, accepting, or blocking. Once you can recognize and understand each of them as they occur, in you and in others, life is going to be less frustrating and *a lot more fun!*

And remember:

Accept everything as an offer.
When in doubt, offer!
If in doubt, you are probably blocking.
and
The more attached you are to "the plan,"
the more likely you are to block.

CHAPTER 5
IT'S ALL ABOUT RELATIONSHIP

"Improvisation means coming to the situation without rigid expectations or preconceptions. The key to improvisation is motion – you keep going forward, fearful or not, living from moment to moment. That's how life is."

\- **Bobby McFerrin**

WHAT'S IT ALL ABOUT?

In improv as in life, everything is about relationship.

Truth be told, not just in improvisation but in acting as well, it is all about relationship. And in life, the same is true. At the end of the day, everything, absolutely *everything*, is about relationship.

And, on the stage, as in life, there are only seven categories of relationship that you are ever engaged in.

THE SEVEN CATEGORIES OF RELATIONSHIP:

1) *YOUR RELATIONSHIP WITH YOURSELF*

It should go without saying that this is the most important of all relationships. It is our first, it is our longest, it is our most constant, and it is our most intimate. And yet, unfortunately, most of us live as though this is the least important relationship. This is the reason we are here on this planet. The quality and clarity of this relationship dictates the quality and clarity of all others. (No pressure, right? Don't worry, we'll get there.) This whole book is actually an exploration of the duality in this relationship: The imaginative, collaborative link between your soul and the person you have shown up as on planet earth. You are both the player and the character. You are both pure source energy and the human expression that it is living in, as, and through. (Again, no pressure.)

2) *YOUR RELATIONSHIP WITH ANOTHER PERSON(S)*

It's very likely that when you read this chapter's title, your first thought was that I was referring to relationships with other people. The danger is that we are easily distracted and overwhelmed by too much attention on those relationships — or should I say that we tend to put too much attention on the *other person's role* in each relationship. Which is not to say that our relationships with other people are not important. Of course they are! They are our primary training ground for the back and forth of offering and accepting. However, it is a rare human being who realizes that their relationship with every other human being is their own responsibility. (Don't panic, we'll come back to that in just a bit.)

3) *YOUR RELATIONSHIPS WITH OTHER LIVING CREATURES*

Humans are not the only beings on this planet, they are a small part of a much bigger world filled with endless unique creatures. They are always offering, just as we are — it just takes more awareness to understand and accept what we are given. When a dog reaches to be pet, when a snake hisses, when a bee lands on your arm, all of these things are offers we can choose to accept or block. And again, whether we believe it or not, the reality is that our relationship with these creatures is 100% our responsibility.

4) *YOUR RELATIONSHIP WITH THINGS*

In these relationships, the thing itself (the object, personal possession, or belonging) is the offer.

Opinions may differ as to what constitutes an object or a thing rather than a living being. For instance, a tree may be a living being to some and an inanimate object to others. But regardless of our personal perspective, the fact still remains that if they are in this category, they are themselves the offer, rather than making an offer. Our relationship, the back and forth between us and the object, is 100% a matter of our choices and therefore 100% our responsibility.

5) YOUR RELATIONSHIP WITH SYSTEMS

As human beings, we naturally seek community. Those communities evolve into systems, groups, and institutions. Since systems are made up as, by, and for people, our relationship with those systems have many of the same qualities as our relationship with other people. And much like our relationship with other people, our relationship with the systems created by people are, once again, our responsibility.

6) YOUR RELATIONSHIP WITH YOUR ENVIRONMENT

Our relationship with the environment has to do with our physical surroundings (whether natural or man-made), nature as a whole, and the world in which we live. Our environment contains elements of the other categories we've discussed. For example, a man-made environment is going to be filled with objects and a natural environment may have a variety of living creatures. Our response to and acceptance of that environment as an offer is often affected by our feelings toward the other relationship types and how that comes together is (you guessed it!) our responsibility.

7) *YOUR RELATIONSHIP WITH THE UNIVERSE*

Your relationship with the Universe is the biggie. No matter what your perspective or what your belief system, this relationship dictates a lot of our ability to respond to, and even comprehend, the other six types of relationships. Historically speaking, humans are prone to believe that all other relationships are indicative of our relationship with the Universe. If things are going well in the other relationships, we are doing well with the Universe — and vice versa. That belief in and of itself is (you know what's coming) our responsibility!

THE SECRET OF THE UNIVERSE

There is one profound and fundamental, yet largely unrecognized, truth that governs our relationship with the Universe. Understanding and accepting this fundamental truth is life altering. It will not only clear up a lot of misconceptions about your relationship with the Universe, but every other type of relationship you have, including your relationship with yourself. And that truth is simply this: The Universe only offers and accepts. It *never* blocks.

In case you missed that, let me say it again:

The Universe **NEVER BLOCKS**!

In other words:

Nothing happens <u>to</u> you. It is all happening <u>for</u> you.

There is truly nothing more important for you to understand and take to heart as you move through the improv of your life.

The Universe is offering, always. We might perceive it as a block because we have an idea of what it *should be* instead of what it *is*.

We've been told this over and over again for millennia. We just haven't been listening.

> *"Ask, and it shall be given you; seek, and ye shall find; knock, and it shall be opened unto you:*
> *For every one that asketh receiveth; and he that seeketh findeth; and to him that knocketh it shall be opened."*

> > \- Matthew 7: 7-8

This is the greatest single piece of wisdom that the metaphorical, metaphysical guide can offer you: the Universe is always offering you opportunities and unconditionally accepting the offers that you make. Once we wrap our head around that, we are truly freed from the fear of random possibilities.

Or as our friend Mr. Einstein is said to have put it:

> *"The most important decision we make is whether we believe we live in a friendly or hostile universe."*

Think of the Universe as the most giving and forgiving improv partner you will ever have.

DANCING WITH YOURSELF

Usually what we perceive as the Universe blocking us is, in fact, us blocking ourselves.

As Mr. Shakespeare said, "All the world's a stage." *All* the world, not just that part where you are interacting with others. All of it, including the time when you are seemingly alone. Humans are in a state of constant interaction — a continual dance of offering, accepting, and blocking, and when we are not dancing with someone or something else, we are dancing with ourselves.

In an improv, the audience only knows what is said and done by each of the performers. In life, you are dealing with what is said and done by others, what is said and done by you, *and* you are aware of and interacting with your own thoughts.

Even when you are alone, you are still in an improv with yourself. You are still making a series of offers, you are still blocking and accepting as you so choose. The problem is that most of the time when you are self-blocking, nobody in the whole entire world knows it, not even you. It goes unnoticed because it is unconscious. But if it makes you feel any better, you are definitely not alone. Virtually everyone else on the planet is busy unconsciously blocking themselves, too.

Self-blocking is what we do every time we say "no" to ourselves. Every time our mind, our spirit, our essence makes an offer, we are likely to have a default block, based on whatever preset gets triggered. If we do manage to bypass the immediate "no," it is extremely likely that our alternative is to roll out the subtle, underhanded block of "Yes, *but*…"

Now, it's not that every thought is beautiful and potential genius, but every thought is an offer if you allow it to be. And if you practice accepting your mental offers long enough, you will reach a point where the world around you seems more open, more friendly, and more willing to accommodate your hopes, dreams, and desires.

I'M BORED!

Once upon a time, just a few years back, I was doing a residency at a charter school teaching creativity to classes of 7th and 8th graders. It was a wonderful experiment and the kids, who were thrown into the newly created class without warning, basically fell into two essential camps: those who were excited and wanted to "get it right" and those who were fearful (whether they recognized it or not) and so acted out.

By the end of the first day, about 80% of the students were won over and really into the playful experiment. In the 20% that were not completely convinced of the fun they could have if they decided to join in wholeheartedly, there was one student in particular (we'll call him Sam) who made quite a show of being above it all. He was a bit of a joker and clearly one of the "cool kids" with every intention of staying that way.

My class was an open affront to most of what was considered standard "cool" stuff. So one day about a week into the eight week class, we were all sitting on the floor discussing an exercise in sensory awareness that we had just finished. All of a sudden, this cool young man burst out with *"Ugh! I'm so bored!"*

Without a pause, I turned to him with a smile and said, *"Sam, if you are bored, that's your soul calling you out. That's on you. Make an offer. Don't waste one second of your life being bored."*

Then I invited his classmates and him to start throwing out random offers. Once he got over the shock of being called out as responsible for what he had fully intended to blame me for, he quickly turned around. It took him awhile, but six weeks later, Sam (and honestly, all of his classmates) had become remarkably good at offering, accepting and rarely, if ever, blocking.

The important takeaway here is, Sam is not alone. We all know what it's like to feel bored. Often what we express as "bored," is a feeling of stagnation, frustration, limitation, or lack of clarity or purpose. All of which can be solved by the one person we are always with: ourselves. Once again, it's quite simple.

When we get that feeling, it's not an excuse to feel bad, it's a signal to make an offer.

SECRET OF THE UNIVERSE (PART 2)

We know that the Universe never blocks and here's the flip side to that truth — only humans block intentionally.
Let me say that again:

Only humans block intentionally.

Meaning, humans, animals, or systems might block you inadvertently by getting in the way of what you want, but blocking intentionally? Only humans do that.

In other words, when you are feeling that something, anything, is blocking you, it has to be a human.

And here's another in a long line of blindingly obvious newsflashes: though other people can block you, the person that you are with more often in your lifetime than anyone else *is you*! So statistically speaking, most of the time when you feel that block and you know it has to be a human, simple logic will tell us that it's probably *you*.

When you feel like something is blocking you, odds are it's probably you.

OUR RESPONSE-ABILITY

You might remember me saying this at the top of the chapter:

> However, it is a rare human being who realizes that their relationship with every other human being is their own responsibility. (Don't panic, we'll come back to that in just a bit.)

OK, we're coming back to it.

We have 100% responsibility for everything in our lives. Whenever I say this, it often makes clients, students, friends, and essentially anyone who hears it either nervous or defensive. The idea of being 100% responsible for their life immediately makes most people want to jump to their own defense and let me know that they cannot possibly be at fault or to blame for everything that happens in their life.

And just in case it did that to you, let me be super-duper absolutely clear, once and for all:

Being 100% responsible for everything in your life does not have anything to do with fault or blame.

Fault and blame are judgments. They are labels that are often a form of blocking. Responsible is neither fault nor blame, it is taking ownership of the moment, if you will.

Being responsible in this context has to do with being response-able. We have the *ability to respond* however we choose to everything in our lives.

We are not only 100% responsible for our lives, but we have a 100% response-ability in our lives. Remember that our experience is not based on the offers we receive, but on the offers we make.

I'm glad we had this talk.

RELATIONSHIPS AND STATUS

In the 1980's when I studied improv at the National Theatre of Great Britain, I was introduced to Keith Johnstone's concept of what he calls "status transactions."

When most of us hear the word status, we think of status as synonymous with terms like class or social standing. But status in the Johnstone sense is not limited to social standing, but rather includes all relationships of any kind and the status of each individual in that relationship.

Status interactions occur in any relationship. Not only relationships between two people, but every one of the seven types of relationships are given to status interactions.

Status interactions are happening constantly and, more likely than not, unconsciously. We have feelings about where we fit in various circumstances relative to others, and we make assessments, judgements, and decisions about others based on the feelings that we get.

Your perception of your status in any relationship, at any given moment, dictates what you deem to be acceptable in terms of the offers you might make, the offers you accept, and the offers that you block.

STATUS INTERACTIONS

In any status interaction, your offers can do 4 things:

- Raise your status
- Lower your status
- Raise the other's status
- Lower the other's status

That's it.

Everything you do in every relationship is already doing at least one of those things at any given moment. Now it's time to become conscious of it.

We are feeling things and doing things in response to our status interactions all the time. Actors use this as a tool to play and you can as well.

PERCEPTION AND FEELING

Status on the stage is in the purview of the audience. Status in life is a matter of perception and it both comes from and causes us to feel positively or negatively about ourselves in relationship to others. Our status triggers behavior, both positive and negative. Our status behavior is often triggered by feelings around control and need. In generalized terms, the person with the most control is perceived or felt to have the highest status, while the person with the greatest need is perceived to have the lowest status.

However, even in cases where the situation or circumstance would seem to be placing people in a particular status, their expressed attitude about the situation and their behavior can profoundly affect their status in relationship to those around them.

For instance, we might assume that a king would have high status. But if that king happened to be, say... Louis XVI, then his high status was definitely not accepted by those around him (proven in great detail by the French Revolution).

The reverse may also be true. Think about Mother Teresa, who had no conventional social standing whatsoever in terms of money, a home, or most things people give value to, and yet due to her compassion, she has a status that is considerably higher than most other humans.

NOT GOOD OR BAD

When people start working with status, there is often a misconception or bias that tends to evolve. They will, often unconsciously, think that high status is good and low status is bad or vice versa.

The stereotypical preconception might be that high-status people are bossy, pushy, or arrogant, and that low-status people are weak, stupid, or needy. Conversely the preconception might be that someone of high status is super smart, benevolent, or confident and that someone of low status is gentle, quiet, and humble.

But status is relative. And the status of a character is circumstantial. It goes up and down relative to the other person or people they are with and what their situation and circumstances are. Status is not an inherent personality characteristic.

STATUS IS RELATIVE

I have a client, Ava, who is in a very high-status profession. In her work, she was often having to deal with a great deal of conflict. For quite some time, she had come to believe that she could relieve the conflict for the other person by lowering her own status below theirs. She would deliberately lower her status to make the other person feel better. But there was a big problem with that.

Lowering her status backfired, because when she needed the other person to hear her or respect her opinion, she had already given away the status in their relationship by making the other person feel they were right and that any conflict was hers to either correct or acquiesce to.

What Ava had really meant to do was to alleviate the conflict. The difficulty happened when she lowered her status rather than raising the other person's.

Simply opting to lower her status and get it below the other person's status in an attempt to relieve the conflict may have stopped the hostility of the moment, but it also led the other person to believe that they were always right and she was always wrong.

STATUS ON THE SUBWAY

Imagine a packed subway car.

A grungy and dirty person sitting in one of the seats on that subway car may have low status. The people sitting next to that person may be really reluctant to do so, but the need or desire for the seat causes them to sit anyway. Therefore, the seat has high status.

But the moment that same person smiles at the pregnant person standing, gets up, and gives them their seat, their status goes up.

Their status goes up because of their kindness. It goes up because of their willingness to inconvenience themselves and give up the seat (which, as we established, has high status). And it goes up in relationship to the people who chose to sit and did not offer their seat to the pregnant person.

STATUS AND YOUR RELATIONSHIP
WITH YOURSELF

You would think that in terms of status, our relationship with ourselves would be fairly straightforward, but it's actually a multilayered status interaction.

There is the way we perceive, feel about, and/or interact with:

- The conscious self we intentionally show the world
- The unconscious self that shows up anyway
- The soul
- The physical body
- The ego

We may feel worthy, passive, powerful, trustworthy, unreliable, capable, or incapable and each of these feelings will affect the way we treat ourselves and the way we present ourselves to others. It can also affect the way we treat others or allow them to treat us.

Most people have a default or habitual status. Their natural habit in the majority of interactions is to either "play" high-status or low-status. Most people tend to be unaware of their default status, but once we become aware of it, it can be very empowering. Simply knowing where you are comfortable can help you recognize your presets and your knee-jerk reactions.

Once we learn about status interactions, the goal is to become fluid and be comfortable at either end of the spectrum and anywhere in-between. We need to become aware of our default status so we are not victimized or controlled by it.

HABITUAL STATUS PLAYERS

Many of our presets began early in life. We learned to play a certain status habitually because it seemed, to our unconscious self, to get us what we wanted.

We might play low-status because that is the way we feel most safe, unobtrusive, inoffensive, or kind. It might feel like that is the way to incur the least judgment or negative reactions from others.

We might habitually play high-status because we can feel helpful, strong, safe, or powerful. A habit of playing high-status is also a way of blocking any perceived challenges.

Status habits can be tricky to change, once set in place. They essentially become traits of our personality.

DUNCAN AND LEILA

Also in the late 80's, I was teaching the same group of actors for several semesters in a progressively more intense sequence of improvisation classes. These actors became quite adept at improv and were fearless at leaping into any exercises that I could come up with.

But in this group of highly skilled players, two of my best had a problem. No matter what I tried, they could not step out of their habitual status to save their lives. This was not for a lack of skill or understanding or even willingness to try — they simply could not perceive their own habitual status.

One student, Duncan, was a habitual high-status player, while his friend and classmate, Leila, was a habitual low-status player. When I would place them in an improv and ask them to shift their status to something other than their habit state, they simply could not do it. They would try, God-love-them, but they would always fail profoundly and often unintentionally hilariously.

If I asked Duncan to lower his status, he would inevitably obliterate his partner's status. If I asked Leila to raise her status, she would accidentally raise the status of her partner with speed and precision.

For many months, I could not make a dent in their understanding. Then one day, I had the wild idea to put them in an improv together and have them imitate *each other*.

Miraculously, Duncan had low status, gentle and gracious, and Leila had high status, gregarious and in charge. When I would ask Duncan to lower his status further, he could do it instantly and effortlessly. When I asked Leila to raise her status, she too could do it without hesitation.

Their classmates and I were stunned, while both of them had a realization that stuck with them thereafter and completely changed their understanding of themselves and their interactions with others not just in improv, but in their daily lives.

HEALTHY STATUS INTERACTIONS

Healthy relationships have what I would call fluid status interactions. No one is stuck in one position or another, but takes on whatever status the interaction calls for at that moment. Both parties are comfortable being high or low-status at any given time and the status fluctuates naturally depending on the subject.

For instance, in a marriage that is healthy, neither partner has to always be in a high-status position—they don't have to always be right, always have the answer, or always be in control. Likewise, it is safe for them to take on a low-status position when they need to without feeling less than their partner. They can be vulnerable without fear that it will lessen their partner's opinion of them or put them at a disadvantage in any way.

Think of status interactions like a teeter totter. One side has to be down for the other to be up. Trading positions takes effort, but the most effort is expended when the two sides are in complete balance. Balance requires cooperation and intention between both parties.

Understanding status interactions can have a great impact on all of your relationships. Remember that, just like offering and accepting, what you do with your status and what you do to anyone or anything else's status is a choice—and therefore 100% your response-ability.

Lovely how this all fits together, isn't it?

STATUS OFF-STAGE

I love teaching status to actors, but by far my favorite place to teach status interactions is in a workshop I call "The Art of Creative Negotiation." I teach this workshop to parents who are struggling to advocate for their child in the special education system.

Parents in that position generally are stressed out beyond belief and feel as though everyone in the system holds the fate of their child in their hands. Oftentimes, their status has been obliterated repeatedly in their struggle to get help for their child. They end up feeling like the uninvited guest in a game where everyone else knows the rules but them. School administrators, social workers, doctors, therapists, and teachers all seem to have an inherent higher status in this process than they do.

And it's not just the parents whose status gets lowered — often the status of the child at the center of the negotiation gets completely negated or ignored.

Once I've introduced the concept of status, I put the parents into improvisational scenarios so that they can start to feel what it's like to intentionally work with status. They enjoy the feeling of consciously shifting status and see the negotiation as a game that they can win, as opposed to one they hate playing. The transformation in these beleaguered parents is heartwarming, but the real magic occurs when they are introduced to a wonderful technique of altering the status of something off-stage.

Actors in an improv can raise and lower the status of themselves and the other players, as well as anything on the stage and the stage space itself. But the status interactions are not limited to those people and things actually present on the stage. An actor can raise or lower the status of something or someone who is offstage by treating them with reverence or disdain.

In the case of these parents, the "something offstage" is the child. The children whose fate, education, diagnosis, or resources are being negotiated are rarely in the room, and as I said, their status often evaporates in the shadow of the systems on which they are dependent. All I do is show the parents how to raise the status of the child offstage, by constantly bringing the child's needs, desires, and strengths into the forefront of the conversation.

As the child's status becomes reanimated, so does the status of the parents. As the parents begin to feel their status rise, so does their energy, their sense of hope, their confidence, and their feeling of control.

The entire room full of tired, frustrated, worn-down parents whose ability to help their child has been swallowed by the system can suddenly understand the dynamics of status in their advocacy conversations and they light up like Christmas trees.

It's not just their new skill of status interactions that is causing their joy, it is the simple act of raising the status of their off-stage children. And along with their children rising in everyone else's perspective, the parents are raised up as well, because as parents, they hold a connection to that now high-status child that is singular and unique.

They are the parent of that amazing child! They are no longer the beggar at the table. They are mom, they are dad, they are second in status only to the unique creative genius that is their child.

STATUS INTERACTION VS STATUS MANIPULATION

In 1986, I was a brand-new teacher at the National Shakespeare Conservatory, when two of my former teachers, current coworkers, and I'll admit, heroes, asked me to join them on a new and exciting project. They were teaching acting and voice to attorneys and they invited me to join them and teach improvisation.

I agreed whole-heartedly and jumped right in. Even though I had been a skilled and trained improviser for years, this was the first time I was going to be *teaching* improv to anyone.

My new students were more than ready to learn the concepts that I'd used for years and take them into the real world. I taught them offering, accepting, and blocking, and they marveled at the applications in the courtroom as well as with their clients and colleagues.

And once I had introduced them to the basics, I was also gung-ho to teach them my newfound love: status.

I had a great time, and so did they, experimenting with status interactions in improvised scenarios of negotiations and trials. It was great to explore and experiment, but it didn't take long before I began to question the power I was giving to these people. Because I realized that perhaps a better name for status interactions in this context was status manipulation.

In a courtroom, there actually is an audience of a judge or a jury or both. It's a strange combination of both real life and theater. By teaching these attorneys to manipulate the status of the people in the room, I felt as though I might be opening a Pandora's box. Not because status manipulation is inherently bad, but it is a technique that can potentially be used against someone without their awareness.

I got really uncomfortable, worrying that I was teaching these attorneys techniques for manipulation.

And in a way, I was—in the same way that teaching someone to drive a car is also teaching them to run a red light. The potential is there, but if they actually follow all the rules, that is not going to happen.

You see, there are fail-safes in the system. Manipulation is only possible if you are not, first and foremost, offering and *accepting.* Manipulation means that you are disregarding the other person's offers and moving the interaction solely toward your planned result.

You can't really learn status interactions without first learning to offer, accept, and not block. And you can't be good at those without conquering your attachment to your planned outcome or the response you want your partner to give.

You can certainly try to diminish someone's status while blocking their offers, but you are going to come across as a bully and a tyrant. You can also try to diminish someone's status to force things to turn out the way you have planned, but you will come across unsympathetic, uncaring, arrogant, and (here's a shocker) *manipulative*!

I discovered very quickly that, just like with an actor on a stage, an attorney in a courtroom, a teacher, a parent, or a partner who tries to force or manipulate their status interactions without regard to "in improv as in life" will only find themselves frustrated, cranky, bored, boring, and potentially very lonely.

THE IMPACT OF PRESETS

What we offer, what we accept, what we block, our attitude toward relationships, and our perception of our status is all directly related to our presets.

Remember:

We all have "presets" built into our thinking based on either our interpretation of the feedback we got from our previously expressed ideas or our interpretation of the feedback we witnessed others receiving for theirs.

Once upon a time, way back in the 1980's (clearly a busy decade for me), I was visiting actor friends, David and Nancy Lee-Painter and their two little girls, Allix and Molli, in Seattle. It was on a super busy morning when all the adults in the house were late and in a big hairy hurry to leave the house when Nancy was met with this scenario:

Three-year-old Allix had the wonderfully creative idea to color all over the face and hands of her one-year-old sister Molli with markers. As Nancy came down the stairs, she was met with the glowing face of her brightly colored toddler and the even more glowing face of her super proud older sister.

With that enviable childlike wonder Allix announced, *"Mommy, look!"* unveiling the spontaneous artistic impulse that she had followed with great care to what she and Molli clearly viewed as its glorious conclusion.

In the world of presets, this is a linchpin moment. From this moment forward, Nancy or any mom's reaction to an event like this establishes a preset that will affect us for the rest of our lives.

Now, imagine yourself in little Allix's position and let's take a look at three ways Mom's reaction might have gone.

1) *"What have you done?!"*
   Your potential presets:
   - I can't trust my ideas.
   - My creativity makes people mad.
   - I'm not safe.
   - I suck.

2) *"That's wonderful!"*
   Your potential presets:
   - My creative impulses are good.
   - I'm safe and free to explore my ideas.
   - Other people's boundaries and safety mean nothing if I have an idea.

3) *"Oh Honey, that's lovely. And next time, let's do it on paper so that we can keep it forever and we don't have to wash it off Sissy."*
   Your potential presets:
   - My creation was valuable, so valuable we need to keep it.
   - It is safe to explore my ideas and build on them to make them better.
   - Other people's boundaries need to be respected.

OK, now let's look at this as an improv. The initial offer that you made was the drawing on your sister. The same potential responses from Mom are noted in terms of offering, accepting, and blocking.

1) *"What have you done?!"* [BLOCKED]

2) *"That's wonderful!"* [ACCEPTED WITHOUT AN OFFER]

3) *"Oh Honey, that's lovely. And next time, let's do it on paper so that we can keep it forever and we don't have to wash it off of Sissy."* [OFFER ACCEPTED AND BUILT ON WITH ANOTHER OFFER]

Now let's look at how the same scenario plays out with the status interactions noted.

1) *"What have you done?!"*
   - Severely lowered your status
   - Assumed ultimate high status of Mom
   - Obliterated status of the creative offering
   - De facto raised the status of your little sister

2) *"That's wonderful!"*
   - Raised your status
   - Raised the status of the artwork above everything, even Mom and her need to get to work
   - Completely obliterated the status of your little sister

3) *"Oh, Honey, that's lovely. And next time, let's do it on paper so that we can keep it forever and we don't have to wash it off of Sissy."*
   - Raised your status
   - Raised the status of the art

- Maintained an equal status between you and your little sister
- Cements Mom's inherent high status by being not only mom, but a safe place and wise teacher

If Mom also includes any necessary safety instructions about the use of markers on Sissy, she can set a pattern of:

- Raising the status of all other people
- Raising the status of safety as a concept
- Raising the status of ourselves in the future

I probably don't have to tell you that Nancy's response was, of course, number three. It was a **HUGE** teaching moment for me. I was not a parent yet and I had only just begun teaching status at the time, but it was like watching a brilliant training video on human interaction.

Now, interestingly enough, Nancy was and is not only one of the most instinctively compassionate parents I have ever met, but she is also an amazingly talented and generous actor. Watching Nancy on the stage is an exquisite experience. Sharing the stage with Nancy is equally wonderful because she is a generous, present moment performer — and clearly that translates directly into her life.

Incidents just like this are one moment in a stream of moments that happen every day. Whether we are the mom or the child, we probably don't realize which moments are going to build into long-term consequences and lasting presets.

There is no knowing what moments are huge and what moments are small until you have long moved past them, so it is best to enter every situation mindful of the potential impact of your choices. It is up to you to be ready to accept everything brought to you and offer, graciously, in return.

AND NOW YOU KNOW

Since everything is about relationship and relationships always have a status dynamic in play, wouldn't it be lovely if every relationship had a healthy status dynamic. Well, now that you know about status, and now that you know about offers, and now that you know that everything in your life is your response-ability, you can consciously create healthy interactions in all the scenes you play on the great stage of life.

OK, that might be a little bit much to ask already, but at least the potential is there. Don't worry, we're not done yet.

We've only just begun to play.

CHAPTER 6
BEHAVING TRUTHFULLY

"Acting is behaving truthfully under imaginary circumstances."

\-   **Sanford Meisner**

THE PLANNED PART

We've spent a great deal of the book so far dealing with how to handle the spontaneous aspect of life (improvisation). Well, now we've arrived at the portion of the metaphor that helps us begin to focus on our approach to the planned, prepared, or anticipated part of life (acting).

I know it might seem like a contradiction—plan, don't plan—but yeah, as I've said before, welcome to life! Remember the cute little ducks? (OK, the ones *I* imagined were cute. Yours might have been annoying, especially if you were late when they stopped traffic, but I digress.)

Point being, it's not our plan that is the issue and it's not our preparation that is the problem, it's our attachment to our expected outcome that bites us in the bottom.

As I said before:

We get a plan, we set our intention, we release our attachment to the expected outcome, and we set about offering and accepting our way to our intended destination.

That, my friends, is a description of every production of every play ever, since well before Mr. Shakespeare. It is also a description of every day of every life ever since the dawn of time.

SO MANY -ISMS

Oh, baby! There are so many acting techniques and concepts that have become my "in acting as in life"-isms over the years that this chapter could easily be 100 pages long. And I promise you that every single viable acting technique or concept has a direct correlation to life.

But since this is not an acting textbook and since my publishers will smack me if I send them a 100-page long chapter, I'll stick with just six of my favorite broader acting concepts that, like with all their fellow acting concepts and techniques, translate directly into life. And the best part is that, just as with improv, you don't have to be an actor to utilize these concepts and techniques to get the brilliance flowing in your life. Woo-hoo!

Let's start here.

IN ACTING AS IN LIFE #1:
IT'S WHAT YOU DO THAT MATTERS

Just as with improvisation, the craft of acting is mired in its own fair share of myths and misunderstandings. Perhaps the grandest misunderstanding about acting is the belief held by many, both actors and non-actors alike, that the whole experience of acting is a self-indulgent practice of the actor following their feelings down an emotional rabbit hole.

Notice that the quote at the beginning of this chapter by the renowned acting teacher Sanford Meisner does not read, "Acting is feeling lots of emotions in imaginary circumstances," or "Acting is thinking a lot about how to justify imaginary circumstances."

The great acting teacher Jimmy Tripp used to say, "*Feeling follows doing.*" In a journal entry from 1984, I wrote down what Jimmy was saying (at the top of his lungs!) in class that day:

"Do something! Anything! But don't sit around waiting to feel. That will come, or it won't, but you still need to throw yourself into the ring. You have to commit! Because, at the end of the day, I don't really care what you feel, I care what the audience feels. It's not about how you feel, it's about the impact of what you do. What is your impact on the world of the play, on the other characters, on the audience? That is what is critical."

In terms of our improv vocabulary, an offer that just stays a thought is no offer. No matter how long you *think* about it or how much you *feel* about it, until you actually *do* something, it's a potential offer at best and a block at worst.

How do we break out of that?

You know the answer!

We offer.

FEELING VS DOING IN LIFE

When actors focus on what they feel, it puts their attention on themselves. Their attention is on how it feels to them, not what they are doing in the moment to add to the story.

Likewise, when we sit around on the couch eating Cheetos and feeling all kinds of feelings about what other people are doing or experiencing, our focus is not really on them, it's on ourselves. We like to talk about how disappointed we are in others that they didn't do something to fix this situation, but what do *we* do?

A lot of us act like novice actors in our daily lives. We mistake feeling for doing. We turn on the TV, we see a tragic news story and we feel bad about what's going on in the world. We think that, because we feel badly, we are connected to what's happening. We think we are participating.

But honestly, so what? You feel bad. And…? What do you do? What *can* you do? Use your imagination and then act on the possibility you envision.

I know, the problems can look profound and you may not be able to save everyone. But that is no reason to do nothing. If you see people in your community are hungry, you can make sandwiches and take them to feed people in the park. Ten sandwiches might not be much, but it's ten people who were hungry but now won't be.

When we get locked up in feeling rather than doing as an actor, we are self-indulgent.

When we get locked up in feeling rather than doing as a human, what are we? Self-indulgent!

Or as the iconic acting teacher Stella Adler put it:

"In life, as on the stage, it's not who I am but what I do that's the measure of my worth and the secret of my success. All the rest is showiness, arrogance and conceit."

THE SOURCE OF THE SOUNDBITES

I've been blessed to study with lots of remarkable acting teachers in my life. But I have noticed over the years that in my teaching, I tend to quote one far more than all the others. That one, is the late, great, Mario Siletti.

Mario was, indeed, memorable. He was this rather dapper, mustachioed, Italian gentleman in a tweed professor's jacket, who was just affected enough that people often thought he was British.

And though his manner was indeed quite memorable, what made him so quotable is the fact that he taught in soundbites. And clearly, it was a very effective mode of teaching because, obviously, the soundbites stuck!

Mario passed away around 1991 and yet hundreds of my students who have never met the man, quote him to this day. He had an iconic phrase for almost every acting challenge imaginable. And so, fasten your seatbelts, you're liable to hear a few. Starting with this one:

"You've got to find the love"

- Mario Siletti

IN ACTING AS IN LIFE #2:
YOU'VE GOT TO FIND THE LOVE

Back in the day, Mario, with his charming affectation in full bloom, would step up in front of the acting class where students had just finished doing an assigned scene or monologue. He would dramatically take one of the student's hands and turn to the class and say:

"Honeys! Kids! Listen to me. Listen to me, kids. I'm going to save your lives! <u>You've got to find the love.</u>"

He meant that, in order to understand why a character gets up in the morning and does whatever it is that they do, what you've really got to understand is, "What do they love?"

A character that robs a bank does it out of love. It may be a love of family, a love of power, a love of freedom, but it is always out of love for something.

A character that kills someone does it out of love. It may be a love for another (revenge), a love of power (to eliminate a threat), a love of country or freedom or ideals (war), or a love of their own life (self-defense).

A character that gets married may be assumed to be marrying out of love for their spouse, but as an actor explores the character, they may discover that what the character truly loves is security, feeling needed, having the American dream, or wanting to appear to "have it all."

Each one of these choices creates different behavior. Imagine the differences between a bride who marries for romantic love versus one who marries for power.

When you know what someone loves, you will know what is causing them to choose the action they are taking.

IN ACTING AS IN LIFE #3:
YOU CAN'T PLAY A NEGATIVE

"You can't play a negative," is another Mario-ism, which means you can't play what you don't want, you can only play what you do want.

You can try. God knows most of us spend a great deal of energy avoiding what we don't want rather than pursuing what we do want. But in acting, if an actor is playing what the character doesn't want, they will be making choices out of fear.

In life, we tend to focus our energy, attention, and our powerful imagination on the things we don't want. We envision the things that might go wrong, what we might lose, and what bad things others might be thinking of us. To put it bluntly, we spend a great deal of time being dishonest in the imaginary circumstances of our lives.

Most of us fail to realize that our imagination is not in charge of what we think. It is a way in which we think. It is a bridge between our divine intention and the life we experience. As actors, we know that our imagination is our tool. As humans, we often become victims of our imagination.

As author Scott Turow said:

> *"Who are we but the stories we tell ourselves, about ourselves, and believe?"*

Most of us put a lot of energy into explaining to ourselves why we can't have what we love, why we won't pursue our passion, or why we can't or shouldn't want our dream.

And when we deny ourselves that love, we end up in fear, frustration, and disappointment.

So how do we turn this around as human actors on the great stage of life? How do we purposefully utilize the imagination to help us achieve our goals? How do we focus our attention on thinking, deciding, and acting as the character we are choosing to play?

In order for an actor to authentically play a character, they must know what the character loves.

In order for you to authentically show up as yourself in your life, you must know what *you* love.

In order to fully show up on this planet as the glorious character we came here to be, do, and share, we must fully embrace the love at the center of our being and work to express it in the most authentic way possible.

IN ACTING AS IN LIFE #4:
YOUR TALENT LIES WITHIN YOUR CHOICE

Even though an underlying premise of this book is that everyone is brilliant, I am by no means suggesting that everything you do is brilliant. You have brilliance inside of you and it is up to you to choose to actively nurture and share that brilliance, rather than just getting by or letting other people's offers take precedence over your own.

Whether it is about accepting an offer from someone else or you making the offer, you are making a choice.

Or as the late great Mario Siletti often said:

*"Your talent lies within your choice."**

And he's right. Any performance is made up of a series of choices. And so is life. It is 100% your responsibility. It is a product of your choices.

*(*Giving credit where credit is due, Mario was paraphrasing his dear friend, mentor, and colleague, the iconic acting teacher Stella Adler.)*

In acting as in life, our choices must be three things:

Specific
Powerful
Positive

We have to make choices about what we do. And the quality of that choice, or if you will, the quality of that offer, determines the success in that moment. In other words, it's not just doing *anything* that is the answer, it's doing something specific, powerful, and positive that contributes to that moment and moves the story forward.

We make a choice from a sea of infinite possibilities based on what we know about the character we are playing and the story we want to participate in. In life, the character you have to know is you and the story that you need to participate in is the life that you are creating. We make a choice about what we want and then we make a choice about how we are going to go about getting it. Then we make an offer.

Without specific choices, an actor just wings it. The performance is happenstance. Without specific intentional choices, life is just happenstance. We are forgetting that life is not happening *to* us, it's happening *for* us. The Universe is offering, unconditionally, in alignment with the offers we are making.

Life is happening for us, to do with as we will.

In our lives, we have been given this glorious role to play and, like any good player, if we make daring, bold, courageous, powerful choices, we will have a breathtaking performance. Likewise, if we make safe, shallow, lazy choices, we will have a boring, uninteresting, soulless performance.

As Ernest Holmes said:

> *"We cannot lead a choiceless life. Every day, every moment, every second, there is a choice.*
> *If it were not so, we would not be individuals.*
> *Nothing is too good to be true."*

IN ACTING AS IN LIFE #5:
IT'S ALL ABOUT MAKING THE OTHER PLAYER
LOOK GOOD

Or as the way it was first drilled into me back in the 80's:

"Acting is all about making the other guy look good."

- just about every acting teacher ever

Think of this as the golden rule on steroids. It's not just "do unto others," but it's the idea that not only are you required to make offers on the stage, you are required to make offers intended to support and enhance the offers of your fellow players.

In acting as in life, when we are primarily concerned with how *we* look, how *we* sound, how *we* are being received, and if *we* are getting what *we* want, then we lose our connection with the present moment and with our fellow players.

Rather than being present, we are either caught in thoughts about the past "What did I just do?" or caught in thoughts about the future "What will they think of what I do?" We are not in the present moment. We are either stuck in the past trying to figure out how to recreate or avoid what has already happened, or we are in the future trying to force something into happening or trying to avoid it.

We are in the past or in the future, or worse yet, both simultaneously. But we are definitely not *here now*.

We are not offering anything to our partners. We are not listening to them. We are blocking them. We are disconnected. We might think we are there with them, it might even look like that to them, but no. We're gone.

What many actors and, you guessed it, many human beings don't realize, is that getting your attention and your energy focused on your partner is what gets the best "performance" out of you. Because when you get your mind off the egocentric perspective of "How do I look?" and put it in the perspective of "How can I help my fellow player(s) look good?" two things happen:

1) Your performance is no longer self-conscious. You are freed from self-judgment and self-critique. You stop feeling and start doing. You focus on your offers and what you can give to the moment.

2) The rising tide raises all boats. By putting your energy into how to help those around you be successful in their efforts, you create more success in each moment that you are a part of. And the better it gets for any of us, the better it gets for all of us. Remember: **Life is not a zero-sum game.**

A GENEROUS ACTOR LISTENS

When an actor is present, listening, aware, accepting, and offering, that is what other actors refer to as "a generous actor." They are there for you. They've got your back. You are safe, supported, heard, and accepted. It feels great to be with generous actors in a production and it feels great to be with those kinds of people in our lives. And yet, on the stage and in life those people can be quite rare.

Actors exist in that strange duality of knowing exactly what words they are going to say and what is expected to happen, while still being available and receptive for the nuances and the spontaneous things happening in the present moment. Remember when I said that it's about planning, preparing, and not getting attached to the outcome? Yeah. That's this.

The stage can become a festival of expectation and we know that expectation is the death of spontaneity. Assumptions and expectations can put actors into a state of autopilot. They know what is "supposed to happen" and

what they want to happen and what they expect to happen, and they block anything that is not that.
Such is life.

We humans don't listen. Not because we have a script (at least not one that is written down), but because we have expectations, and a lot of them.

There's this old actor joke about the way bad actors "listen." These actors are only focused on their lines, their moment, often to the detriment of everyone around them. If you could see inside the head of the bad actor during a scene, it would look like this:

OTHER ACTOR: *Blah blah.*

BAD ACTOR: *My line.*

OTHER ACTOR: *Blah, blah di blah.*

BAD ACTOR: *MY LIIIIIIINE!!!*

(*read with vibrato and full crescendo)

That is what a selfish actor is doing. Unfortunately, it's also what most of us are doing at some point during every day of our lives.

"Listen with your gut, not with your head."

- Sanford Meisner

When we listen from a place of what we expect to hear, we don't really hear the nuances of what is being said, nor do we recognize the emotional truth behind what is being said, either to us or by us.

IN ACTING AS IN LIFE #6:
NEVER, NEVER, NEVER

One more Mario-ism that I always share with my students is:

*"Never explain and never complain
in your life or in your art... both are boring."*

And yet as human beings, so much of what we do during a day is complaining or explaining.

Remember that boring means we are not offering. My student Sam taught us that if we are bored, that's on us, because we are not offering into our own lives.

Well, the same goes for being boring. It's on us. It's usually because we think we are offering when we aren't. This is always the case with explaining and complaining.

Think of it this way: complaining and explaining are not offers, they are simply comments on past offers. Which makes them blocking.

Actors are always striving to find the truth in the present moment. As human beings seeking a spiritually enlightened perspective, we are always striving for a connection, an awareness of the present moment.

If you find yourself complaining or explaining, you are no longer in the present moment. Full stop. Your attention is focused on the past.

In Mario's language, the reason they are boring is because they are inactive. Complaining and explaining are not doing anything except feeding our ego. They do not expand our character, nor do they expand our world. They are boring because they are negative, self-indulgent choices.

Sometimes we legitimately need to explain. Sometimes in order to have everyone understand what is happening in the present moment, we need to acquire context or additional information. This contextual information is always based in the past. It's what playwrights and actors refer to as exposition.

Bad exposition is that which merely explains. Well-written exposition is interwoven with the story. It is not only filling in the gaps, but it has to happen. It has to be shared in that moment because it is part of what is necessary in order to fully experience that moment in the story and in life. When the act of sharing the exposition causes growth in the character/our character and forward movement in the story/our life, then there is a need.

As to complaining? Yeah, I'm going to go out on a limb here and say we *never* need to do that.

Take it from Buddha,

> *"Do not dwell in the past, do not dream of the future, concentrate the mind on the present moment."*

CHAPTER 7
EMBRACING THE OBSTACLES

"The greater the obstacle,
the more glory in overcoming it."

- **Molière**

IN ACTING AS IN LIFE #7

OK, I know that last chapter I told you I was going to be sharing six of my favorite "in acting as in life -isms." Well, this is my favorite, *favorite* -ism, so much so that I'm devoting an entire chapter to it because it is earth-shatteringly important.

Stop for a second and imagine your life without any of the challenges. That would be boring and stagnant. Challenges are inspiration in disguise. Welcome the challenges and use them to inspire, create, and live life to the fullest.

That's this whole chapter in a nutshell.

And if I thought that was all it took to wake us up to the beauty in obstacles, then I'd stop right here.

But umm… I think I'll offer this instead.

IN ACTING AS IN LIFE #7: OBSTACLES ARE WHAT MAKES IT ALL WORTH DOING

Ask an actor what kind of role they like to play. I guarantee you they won't say, "A boring person who always gets exactly what they want and doesn't have any struggles."

In a play, screenplay, or video game, if you don't have an obstacle, you don't have conflict. If you don't have conflict, you don't have anything interesting to experience.

Striving is interesting. Growing is interesting. Even struggling is interesting. Striving, growing, and struggling don't happen without obstacles to overcome.

Think about it. Nobody wins an academy award for playing a role that faces no conflict or writing a script where nothing is overcome. When we play a character in a video game, we pick a game that has a challenge. It is the overcoming of that challenge that's the fun part of playing the game. That experience is cathartic, it stretches our muscles, and it's fun.

In games, we learn to problem solve by solving problems that are simple at first. When we are young, we all play tic-tac-toe. And then we learn that, once both players know the rules, it will always be a tie. Once we realize that there are no more obstacles, we quit playing. It's not fun anymore because there is nothing to overcome. There is no chance that we might lose. There is no obstacle. We know how it's going to turn out.

There is no success because there is no chance of failure. Chew on that one for a moment.

We don't go to the movies to watch a villain give up before he gets started or watch Lassie have no struggle telling people that Timmy fell into the well. Seriously, if Lassie suddenly could talk and tell the people Timmy was in the well, it would be bizarre for a second, but it would take the opportunity to overcome the obstacle, and therefore the interest, out of the story.

Just as if a mega creepy villain like Michael Meyers suddenly took off the mask and called a crisis hotline. Umm… movie over.

We go to the movies or to a play to watch people try to overcome the obstacles that they face. Sometimes they succeed, sometimes they don't, but we will go to watch them try.

Likewise in life, few, if any, of us strive for a job that will be the same every day for the next 40 years, with nothing to learn and no chance for growth or change. Even in our relationships, we don't choose people who always agree with us, always do the same thing every day, and avoid any obstacles.

In life, if there is no obstacle, if there's no chance of losing, there's no point. The transcendence of the obstacle is what gives it meaning.

And yet, even though we agree that obstacles are necessary to find something or someone worthy of our time and effort, most of us think that when we have a problem, it's automatically a bad thing. If something is making it hard to get what we want, that's bad. Right?

IT'S ALL GOOD

Believe it or not, even as much of a Pollyanna as I am, I've had problems with the new age-y phrase, "It's all good!" for as long as I can remember. Not everything that happens in our lives feels good. So, to be clear, I'm not suggesting that for a second.

Accepting everything as happening *for us*, rather than *to us*, does not mean that it's 24/7 sunshine and roses. The obstacles and challenges that we face in life are sometimes very, very hard to characterize as "good." It's when we get stuck in trying to label it as good that we miss the point.

Obstacles and challenges don't have to be easy or happy or something we would categorize as good to be perfect opportunities for the further expression of our brilliance.

If we trust the fundamental concept that this is a benevolent Universe that is always offering, then it is our judgment of the situation that creates the perspective of good or bad. Our *expectation* of what we want or think we want the offer to be is what makes us think of it as good or bad.

Our friend, Mr. Shakespeare said it quite clearly several hundred years ago.

> *"...for there is nothing either good or bad, but thinking makes it so."*

> - William Shakespeare, *Hamlet* (2.2.268-270)

There are many ways throughout the millennia that humankind has tried to grapple with or explain the fact that some things happen which seem harsh or hard. We hear people say, "it's God's will" to explain the seemingly unexplainable.

The problem with the "it's God's will" explanation is that it puts us in the victim position of simply enduring the experience, rather than in the response-able position of having to accept the offer and make our offer back.

Or as Jesus put it a couple of thousand years ago:

"It is done unto you as you believe."

- Matthew 8:13.

No matter who says it or how they said it, the fact is this. And I want you to say it with me:

The Universe only offers.

We are the ones who establish the form and effect of that offer based on what we believe. What we believe not only guides our acceptance or blocking of what the Universe offers, but what we offer in return.

THE IMAGINATIVE RESPONSE

This is where our imagination comes into play. If we have accepted that each and every happening is an offer and we look at seemingly negative happenings with the sure and certain knowledge that there is a gift, a lesson, and an opportunity for us within that offer, then with our imagination we can begin to play with the possibilities of what that gift might be.

Remember that the imagination is the playground of the soul. Therefore, when we allow our imagination to play with the possibilities, we are allowing our souls to communicate directly with us.

Because, again, there is no such thing as a failure of imagination. Sometimes we are just unwilling to allow our imagination to explore certain possibilities because they seem challenging or unlike what we planned. But the trick is to know that if you choose not to pursue it, you are the one responsible for the road not taken. Your imagination did not fail you; you chose not to use it.

If we accept that nothing happens to us and everything happens for us, then we can accept that obstacles are here to help us grow.

The miracle, the inspiration, the growth, and the fun comes from pushing against and working around the obstacles.

"A smooth sea never made a skilled sailor. "

- Franklin D. Roosevelt

BLOCKING VS OBSTACLES

Every block is an obstacle, but every obstacle is not a block.

Almost everything that happens in life that we think of as an obstacle is not a block. It is an offer. It is an opportunity.

Anytime we feel like an obstacle has been set in our path by the Universe, we know that it is not a block. The universe is never trying to stop you. It is never trying to hurt you. It is never trying to make you pay for something. It is offering you an opportunity to step in and make an offer back.

If we can look at every obstacle as an offer, we will treat it differently. Because what do we do with offers? We accept them.

STEPPING INTO THE OBSTACLE

As actors, we don't back away from our obstacle; we look for our obstacle. We use the obstacle to help us determine what our character truly wants and to help us determine the clearest action or tactic to help us overcome that obstacle.

As actors, when faced with an obstacle, we make our choices in terms of it, rather than pretending it's not there or ignoring it. It would be ridiculous if an actor pretended like the obstacle in a play was not there. We all know it's supposed to be there. It's there for the express purpose of letting the characters try to deal with it.

But in life, we get confused. In life, it's not uncommon for us to do just the opposite. We try to ignore our obstacles and pretend they're not there, instead of working *with* them.

When faced with an obstacle, we can either retreat from the obstacle or ignore it entirely, or we can see it for what it is: an offer and opportunity to grow.

DON'T PLAY THE OBSTACLE

It's almost inevitable that once actors start embracing their obstacles, they get a little too focused on them. Actors make choices when they begin approaching a role. They choose their objective, which is what the character wants or needs. They choose their actions, which are the moment-to-moment active choices that help them go about getting what they want. And they identify their obstacles, which are whatever is in the way of what the character wants.

Every once in a while, I will be in rehearsal with an actor who plays the character from a very negative place. They get their obstacle and their objective confused. They start pointing their performance toward the obstacle or crisis and everything gets really dark, fatalistic, and oftentimes boring for the audience because there is no hope in the performance. They focus so much on the obstacle and base all their choices on it.

It's the equivalent of when you are biking or rafting, and you point to the rock you don't want to hit. Now you are most definitely going to hit that rock. You've guaranteed it. That's why rafting guides point to where they want the team to paddle, not to the obstacle they want the team to avoid.

If we put all our focus on the obstacle, we will just keep smashing into it. You have to focus on what you want, not on what you don't want.

FEAR AS AN OBSTACLE

My beloved theater mom Olympia Dukakis always said:

"Fear is boring."

Which I have always interpreted to mean: Fear *makes us* boring.

We acknowledged earlier that fear causes blocking. That's because we make a choice, consciously or unconsciously, to let fear dictate our response to a situation and we choose to block. We try to be safe, we block, we don't offer, and we stay right where we are: boring and bored and letting fear run our lives.

But, if we treat fear as an obstacle, then, by our definition of an obstacle, now we must see fear as an offer!

Uh-oh, what?!

Yes indeed! It is happening for us, not to us. It is there to give us something.

Now it is our response-ability to figure out how we are going to accept it, work with it, and utilize it to help us grow.

See how this works?

We just lost all our excuses because we can always respond. We can always treat every thought, deed, feeling — even fear — as an offer, an opportunity, and a gift.

The weights that you lift to build muscle are not bad. They are there for the very purpose of helping you to build muscle. But you have to pick them up and start working with them, painful as it may be, in order to actually build any muscle. If you do not treat them as an offer, they will lay there and do nothing. Fear, like the weights, is nothing more than something to be utilized to help you grow by overcoming it, not by ignoring it or running from it.

The point is that fear leaves us stuck.

And as David Newman of *Do It! Marketing* says:

"Stuck is voluntary."

PEOPLE AS OBSTACLES

One of the most common things we run from are the people we perceive as obstacles. In a play, the central character is the protagonist and the character who is their primary human obstacle is the antagonist.

Many of us learned a watered-down version of this relationship at some point in grade school or junior high. We were taught that the antagonist is the "bad guy" and the protagonist is the "good guy." But that is a massive oversimplification that, both in a play and in our lives, can make the story frustrating, boring, and predictable!

The antagonist is, simply put, the character whose needs and wants are in direct conflict with those of the protagonist. If you are the protagonist of your own life, then it is your own needs and wants that drive the story, not the antagonist's.

Have you ever heard somebody say, "Life isn't a fairytale"? They're usually talking about how no one is handed a happy ending. But can you think of one fairytale where the protagonist dances through life with no antagonist in sight? Cinderella has her stepfamily. Hansel and Gretel have a witch with questionable taste in building materials. Jack has a giant at the top of a beanstalk. Every one of these protagonists had to overcome the obstacles of their antagonists.

In your life, the key is to recognize that the antagonist is not blocking you, they are giving your story obstacles. If you allow the antagonist's obstacles to help you, then you are learning and growing. The antagonist is doing their job in your life. But when you allow their needs to drive your story, that's when problems occur.

HABITUAL BLOCKERS

All of us have habitual blockers in our lives—you know who they are. The first thing they will tell you is why you can't or shouldn't do something, or why they did or didn't succeed at something.

Habitual blockers are very attached to their limiting beliefs and they are most comfortable if we share them. They believe that their limiting beliefs are universal. Whatever their negative presets taught them to believe or to fear that they could not likely be, do, or have applies to everyone. They usually also believe that life happens to us, not for us. They feel as though the control of their lives is outside of them, and they share that feeling with all those around them.

We have all known habitual blockers in our lives. Maybe some of us have even been habitual blockers.

Not to overstate it, but habitual blockers are dangerous to themselves, to others, and to every form of relationship on the planet. Yeah, glad I didn't overstate it. The reason they are dangerous is because they are actively engaged in contradicting the miraculously natural process that we came here for:

- pursuing our passions
- expressing our spontaneous brilliance
- accepting everything in life as an offer for the benefit of our experience, growth, and evolution

Habitual blockers are essentially making a life practice out of resisting the idea that everything is an offer. They believe that the Universe is playing whack-a-mole with our hopes and dreams. They see the Universe as responsible for every challenge, consciously and deliberately blocking their ultimate happiness.

If you are faced with a habitual blocker, don't take it personally. They haven't singled you out. They generally practice it in every aspect of their lives. Habitual blockers not only block themselves, they block those around them. They assume everyone else and everything else is blocking as actively as they are.

Habitual blockers are what my friends Debra Poneman and Marci Shimoff, co-founders of *Your Year of Miracles*, call "the negativity committee." Members of the committee are the first to tell you why your dream, idea or innovation is not going to work, and why you probably shouldn't even try. But again, don't take it personally. They are not being hard on you in particular. They are truly in a habitual pattern. Their presets are ingrained, and they are sharing their limiting beliefs as though they are facts that apply to you as well as themselves.

They also have miles of reasons for not trying. Anytime they tried and "failed" is usually because of something or someone that they can point to and blame as being responsible for their lack of success. Habitual blockers often see fault, blame, and burden as interchangeable with responsibility.

All the reasons for blocking that we've already addressed are magnified as they try to protect themselves and everyone around them from the "reality" of their *own* fears. Here are some examples that might sound familiar:

"I just got offered a promotion! It's my dream job!"

"Oh Honey, I just don't want you to be disappointed if it doesn't work out."

—

"I just got offered a promotion! It's my dream job!"

"Just be careful. You know what they say about getting what you wish for. It's probably not going to measure up to what you've imagined it would be."

—

"I just got offered a promotion! It's my dream job!"

"You know that's as far as they are ever going to let you go and we both know you deserve better."

Habitual blockers can:

- Cause us to doubt ourselves and our perceptions
- Instill fears in us we didn't even know we had
- Take us out of the present moment to focus on a painful past or an unknown future
- Reinforce the perspective that things happen to us, not for us
- Set us down a path of protecting ourselves from things that have not happened
- Act like carriers of the disease of complacency — since we'll likely fail, it's best not to try

So when you are faced with a habitual blocker, you have to decide, as Marci Shimoff would say:

"What's the most loving thing I can do
for myself right now?"

If your habitual blocker is someone you love, keep loving them. Understand that they mean well and limit yourself to sharing things with them that will not hurt you if they are contradicted. Turn to someone else for your encouraging response. Or if your habitual blocker is someone that you can just remove from your day-to-day life, you might want to do that. Just thank them for sharing and walk away.

The best thing we can do for a habitual blocker is to treat them with compassion. Again, they are not setting out to hurt us, they are actually trying to help, albeit in a convoluted, destructive, soul-crushing kind of way, but the point is they don't mean to hurt you.

YOUR SACRED FRIEND

And now for the person who *does* mean to hurt you.

Someone who is not just a blocker, but who is actually doing everything they can to cause you harm, this is a person who His Holiness the 14th Dalai Lama would call your "Sacred Friend."

I directed an interactive/improvisational event on compassion for an audience of 8,000 young people with the Dalai Lama in 2006. During that event, His Holiness was asked how he could have compassion for the government and the individual people who chased him out of his own country at 14-years-old upon fear of death. They wanted nothing more than to kill him. They torture his people to this day and would kill him if he tried to return to his homeland even now. His answer was (and I paraphrase):

> It's easy to love someone that is easy to love. It's easy to have compassion and love for a friend. But it's that person whose behavior is so egregious, so painful, that in order to show them compassion, your heart has to grow and evolve to be bigger than the pain that they have caused, the pain that they bring into your life — that person is your sacred friend.

You know the old chestnut that forgiveness is not for the person you are forgiving, forgiveness is something you do for yourself. This is what that means. Releasing the bitterness, anger, and resentment that you have for your "sacred friend," reaching beyond that pain, to live your life freed from that weight, is powerful and empowering.

The opportunity to find compassion for the sacred friends in our lives, releasing the power that they have over us and finding the peace that comes with that, is the gift.

His Holiness was expressing the very nature of the gift in facing an obstacle that can, in no way, objectively seem good, or right, or even tolerable. It's not that the obstacle is good, it's that the opportunity it provides you to grow can result in good. And whatever that thing is — be it compassion, love, strength, courage, empowerment, wisdom, you name it — you just can't get it in a life devoid of obstacles.

OBSTACLES ARE INSPIRATION

Accepting every obstacle, every seeming problem as an opportunity, flips life upside down in a good way. It keeps us in the present moment by taking whatever is happening at face value. What is it that I have to learn from this? What is the gift in this? How do I grow? How do I transcend this to help me get closer to my goal?

Find the love. Fall in love with the challenge. Fall in love with the obstacle.

If it's an obstacle, it's an offer. "Yes, and…" that offer!

"Whatever your fate is, whatever the hell happens, you say, 'This is what I need.' It may look like a wreck, but go at it as though it were an opportunity, a challenge. If you bring love to that moment–not discouragement–you will find the strength is there. Any disaster you can survive is an improvement in your character, your stature, and your life. What a privilege! This is when the spontaneity of your own nature will have a chance to flow. "

- Joseph Campbell

CHAPTER 8
ACCEPTING YOUR ROLE

*"The privilege of a lifetime
is being who you are."*

\- **Joseph Campbell**

OUR TWO SELVES

Remember back in Chapter 5 where we talked about relationship? The most important relationship is our relationship with ourselves. This is the reason we're here on this planet, right? Right.

I know you've heard it said that we are "spiritual beings having a human experience." Or in the language of our metaphor:

We are players experiencing the role of a lifetime.
(pun intended)

Our two selves are the player and the character.

It is that duality of being both player (the soul) and character (the human being) that is the essential, fundamental truth of our existence and the source of sooooo much confusion and struggle within and amongst ourselves.

The problem is that the character we are playing is what we perceive as ourselves. Our personality, body, mind, and ego is what we believe to be us. That is what we are referring to when we say "I" or "Me."

The player, our soul that is showing up on planet earth, in, as, and through this human incarnation — that is who we truly are.

ROLEPLAYING AMNESIA

It's a funny thing about playing this role. As soon as we step into the role, we get amnesia. We forget who we really are, the soul/the player, and we see ourselves only as the human being/the character.

I've spent years watching Shelly, my once and future "teaching toddler," play RPGs (roleplaying video games). She'd sit in front of the television for hours at the start of each game, picking everything from the gender of her character to their hair color, their voice, and even their skill set. She created a character perfectly suited to the story she wanted to experience within the world of the game. She didn't know what challenges her character was going to encounter along the way, and she had to learn how easy or difficult it would be to respond in, as, and through this character to the obstacles she had to face. She had to learn as she went. She grew as a player by growing as a character.

Our souls choose exactly what character they want to play in life. The amnesia that we acquire at birth helps us experience the character fully within our world. As the person we are grows through experience, so too does our true self grow. But if it weren't for the amnesia, we would not experience life as reality, and we would not play the game full out.

In a video game, the players must break through their lack of knowledge and understanding to discover who their character is, quest by quest. And in life, we must strive through a lifetime of quests to break through the amnesia to discover and connect with our soul.

ANOTHER MYTH: LOSING YOURSELF IN THE ROLE

Novice actors and certainly non-actors think that successfully playing a role is reaching the point where you lose yourself in the character. The idea that there is virtue in "losing yourself in a role" is nothing short of insanity. And, side note: there have been a number of actors whose sanity has come into question when they attempted to do just that because they thought that was the goal, to somehow blur the line between themselves and the character.

The ridiculousness of this myth can be highlighted through one simple question. If you were a professional actor in a production that required you to be in a sword fight on stage, would you want the actor you were fighting with to lose themselves in the role or in the moment? Um… yeah, maybe not. In fact, we would all want quite the opposite. You would want the individual playing the role, the actor, the one playing the character to be *very much* in control and at the top of their craft, as would we all.

Just as "oops" is not an acceptable response to accidentally stabbing your castmate in a production where you get caught up in the moment, so too is "oops" not an acceptable response at the end of a lifetime when you look back at all the opportunities you passed up because you got lost in the role you were playing and did not listen to your player self.

So the goal in life is not to lose yourself in this lifetime, but find the connection, and the clear path of communication between your "two selves."

THE ILLUSION OF SEPARATION

Much of the time, we think of our soul as something "other," something away from us, still connected to the divine, but not truly driving the show *here*. But the truth is, that there is no show except for that which our soul came here to experience. Our soul is actively engaged in playing this character as successfully as possible.

That is why the most important relationship that you have in this lifetime is the one between yourself the soul and yourself the human. It doesn't matter what you call it, what matters is that you understand that this relationship is an active relationship.

By active, that is to say, it is ongoing. It is not on pause. Our soul is not standing aside, waiting for us to end our life so that it gets engaged again. That would be like an actor in a play waiting offstage or down the street somewhere, while the character is performing on stage. It sounds ridiculous when we think about it that way. But nonetheless, most of us live as though our soul is other and elsewhere. But umm, no. It is not somewhere else. We do not have to reconnect to it when we die. We are always, always, always connected. The soul is expressing in, as, and through us. There is no us without the soul.

WHO'S FLYING THE PLANE?

Let me sneak in another metaphor for this all-important relationship and how far out of whack our perception of it is.

It's like a plane thinking that it's flying itself and the pilot is just along for the ride. The plane thinks it is in charge of the flight and that the person in the cockpit is just waiting to actually do something when they reach the destination. The plane has no idea where it's going, but it never occurs to it that the pilot might. To the plane, the pilot is an other — it's not a plane therefore it does not have anything to do with the flight.

Just to be super-duper clear: *we are the plane and we are actively ignoring our pilot.*

We think we are in charge of whether we let the pilot do anything during the flight. We think we have to meditate, take a class, join a group, or at least feel a certain ethereal feeling to even be in contact with the pilot. And we're wrong.

Phrases like, "I have a personality," "I have a body," "I have a mind," "I have an ego," and "I have an imagination," are all things we say when describing ourselves. That is the ego talking like it's the pilot instead of part of the plane. These are the characteristics that belong to the character your soul is playing. These are the characteristics that *belong* to you. They are not you. They were chosen *by* you in order to help you play the role of a lifetime.

THE PROTECTIVE PERSONALITY

Dr. Sue Morter, author of "The Energy Codes," refers to the ego as "The Protective Personality." She finds that her clients are more able to accept what she is teaching about the ego if she doesn't refer to it by that name.

When we speak of the ego, it is perceived as a pejorative, as though having an ego is an insult. We all have an ego, just like we all have a mind, a heart, and a personality. We often refer negatively to someone as having a "big ego." But that's like saying someone has an "overactive imagination." There is no such thing in either case. Just as an overactive imagination is a misnomer for someone whose imagination is working extra well, so is a big ego one that is not really big, just working super hard to do what the ego does best: protect us.

Think about it. We learn what to fear, we learn what can hurt, we learn what will cause us pain and the ego does it's best to keep us safe from that. And we block. We block anything that will make us feel pain, fear, unsafe, or anything else we don't want to feel.

That is how we learn to think of ourselves as separate. Separate from the Universe, separate from others, and separate from our own soul. We teach ourselves to feel separate as a way of the ego feeling in control.

Well, the reality is that we can't be separated. But when we feel separation, it's the ego taking over. It's like the autopilot kicks into high gear and starts running overtime, protecting us from things that haven't even happened yet, and likely never will.

We protect ourselves from rejection by never applying. We protect ourselves from broken relationships by not ever having relationships in the first place. We protect ourselves from dying in a parachuting accident by never jumping out of a perfectly good plane.

…OK, that's one I believe in, but back to the point.

OUR PATTERN OF PROTECTION

We get into a pattern of blocking anything that doesn't look safe. It doesn't have to look as obviously unsafe as falling a couple thousand feet. It can simply feel unsafe to our identity. When we feel like our sense of self is threatened, it can be just as frightening as physical danger.

But our soulful self — our true self — is forever asking us to reach and stretch and grow and share our unique creative genius. Because, after all, that is why we are here. But since we have fallen into a pattern of believing that the ego is in charge, we override the callings of our soul. We override the divine nudge to be, do, and share, everything we came here to be, do, and share. We go with the ego's safe choices, letting the plane fly itself and letting the character play the scene without the actor present.

But again, the ego is not a bad thing. It's just not. We incarnate in this lifetime with amnesia. We learn to perceive ourselves and the world around us and our protective personality begins to shape and take charge as a matter of survival. We develop presets and then we start protecting based on our presets. Our ego reinforces the protections by creating justification, explanation, expectation, and validation. All our personal myths explain why it's possible or why it isn't possible to be, do, and have everything we want to be, do, or have.

MY STORY OF WHY

I love a good philosophical debate. It's one of my favorite forms of entertainment. It's like conversational crack for me. So of course, during our 15-year relationship, my life

165

partner Rex and I have had lots and lots of lively debates across the dinner table. Rex is not only a brilliant musician, but a really smart guy who likes to ponder big issues. So yeah, we could really dig into some huge metaphysical, philosophical debates that would last for hours. It's wonderful.

In our early years together, there was just one wrinkle in the process. He and I would get into these big debates, and we would be going back and forth and inevitably I would ask some question that started with, ended with, or contained within it the word, "why."

And Rex would interrupt me with:

> *"There is no why. Why is a non-question.*
> *You can't say it that way. Ask it another way."*

OK, I don't know about you, but when I'm in the middle of a fun and fast-moving intellectual debate, the last thing I want is to have my sentence structure or word choice smacked down. "You can't say it that way"? Oh *really*? Yeah, as you may have guessed, that did *not* exactly go over well.

And when I would try to say that to him, he'd just double down.

> *"Why is a non-question. Ask it another way."*

This would turn our lively, fun debates into a festival of frustration for me. But, in order to keep our conversations going, I would play the game, change my words, and try to find a work around to ask my question. For years, I believed that when Rex pulled that out, it was because he was losing the debate and just wanted to shut me down.

Then one day, literally *years* after the first time Rex said, "There is no why," I was teaching an acting class in which a pair of students were frustrated with a scene and they were looking for the reason why a character did something or other and I heard myself say:

*"Why is unplayable. Don't ask why the character is doing something – that's what they will tell themselves for justification but that won't help you. You have to ask what and how questions. Those are playable. **What** do they truly want or need? **What** is in their way? **What** are you going to do about it? **How** are you going to go about it? Why isn't helpful."*

OH MY GOD! Rex was right!!! (a phrase he loves to hear, by the way)

After years of thinking Rex was just pulling out the "why card" as a way of shutting down the debate if he thought he was losing, I suddenly realized he was absolutely right. He wasn't being a pain; he was being profound. (Well OK, he was being a bit of a pain too, but nonetheless, he was right.)

WHY? WHO CARES?

The ego cares. "Why" is always an ego question. It's justification, validation, and explanation. Why did they do that? Why should I have that? Why is this happening to me? It is an attempt to place blame or responsibility somewhere. It's intended to rationalize or justify something that the ego is wanting or not wanting.

Why is what feeds the ego and makes us live as though the ego has the answers.

Our presets explain the whys in our lives. And our ego *LOOOOOVES* why. Why gives the ego just what it's looking for: justification, validation, and all the other "tion"s that make us feel secure. If we know why, we think we understand. Once we understand, we know what to block to protect ourselves. And when we are challenged or we feel insecure or we fail, we always have our "why" to fall back on.

WHY GIVES US THE JUSTIFICATION TO BLOCK

Our protective personality (read: ego) blocks when we don't have a satisfactory answer to why. And sometimes we block by making up a why. Why is a question that is looking for validation, justification, or explanation, and if we don't have one, we will build one in our imagination, because those are things the ego needs in order to feel safe.

Read that carefully:

Why makes the ego <u>feel</u> safe.
Why is not what we need in order to actually <u>be</u> safe.

For instance, let's say our friend Fritz knocked a chair over and it broke. If we don't know why Fritz knocked the chair over, we perhaps imagine that he had an ulterior motive.

Why did he knock the chair over? If it was an accident, why would he just leave it there? Why would he do that when he knows how much I love this chair?

Maybe he did it on purpose.

Maybe he lied when he said he liked my chair.

Maybe he is making a statement.

Maybe he did it to hurt me. Maybe he's not the person I thought he was. Maybe I can't trust him.

Remember, our limiting beliefs give us the answers for why we can't or won't be, do, or have whatever our negative presets taught us to believe or to fear that we could not likely be, do, or have.

THE UNATTAINABLE WHAT

Sometimes when we are looking for why, it's because what we want is unachievable. Such as, in the chair accident, *what* I want is to have my old chair back. Well, if the chair is destroyed, then getting that particular chair back is impossible. So we search for a why to let us focus on something else. It's an emotional need and leads us to irrational action in pursuit of the unattainable. For instance, we might search for someone to blame and then set out trying to punish them or make them pay because, say it with me:

Why makes the ego *feel* safe.

This is where we get into a need for justice, retribution, payback, and vindication because since we can never have our what, we cannot let go of the why. We need it to set things "right."

We need it to fulfill the why to comfort us for not being able to get our unattainable what.

THE RABBIT HOLE OF EXISTENTIAL WHYS

The big existential whys are notoriously unanswerable. Historically, human beings and their protective personalities have gotten really good at answering unanswerable, existential why's with non-answers.

Why did Fritz have to die in that freak chair-falling accident?

Well, perhaps:

- It was his time
- That chair was jinxed
- It was God's will

It's not that these answers make us feel good, necessarily. But they do give us a certain sense of security knowing that we have *an* answer, even if it's one that doesn't make much sense. We even go so far as to build communities around a shared willingness to accept one of the big whys. Our ego feels good surrounded by other egos that tell us our why is right.

Like-minded humans make our ego feel safe. There is after all, as they say, safety in numbers. Adding numbers to our why gives us validation. Adding numbers to our why's explanation increases our validation. And all that validation provides justification for any and all thoughts, words, and deeds that coincide with the shared why. That's the ego missing the point.

What's interesting is that, though the why's may be the same for a large group of seemingly like-minded individuals, if we dig down, the *what* that each individual in the group is truly seeking will be as singular as their unique genius. It's never a why, it's a what. What do they mean to be, do, have, and share?

And it all comes back to overriding the ego and letting the soul fly the plane.

GET THE FOCUS OFF OF YOU

When an actor in a performance is making choices from the ego, it's all about: *"How do I look?" "Do they like me?" "Will I get a good review?" "Is my wig on straight?"* They are focused on themselves and definitely not in the moment. But we already know that, in order to truly succeed on stage, it's always about making the other player look good. It's about getting your focus off yourself and how you are feeling, and onto what you are doing and how you are helping your fellow players.

Well when the ego gets carried away, thinking it's in charge, those are the first things to go. The focus immediately jumps to us. And we get caught up in protecting against, defending against, and blocking anything that does not feel safe. See, the ego gets confused between helping *us* survive and helping *the ego* survive.

It's a tricky distinction. When we believe that the ego is "us," then life is only about survival, and it feels like a competition to be won or lost. But in truth, we can't lose and we can't fail—not really. Failure is a matter of perspective. It is based on the ego's perspective.

As Robert Allen said:

"There is no failure, only feedback."

We are here to do more than survive; we are here to grow, experience, and thrive.

We can't thrive if we can't step outside ourselves and step outside our egos. We can't thrive if we aren't engaged in actively offering into each and every relationship and moment in our lives. We can't thrive if we are not in a constant *active* relationship with our soulful self.

On the great stage of life, our job is to play the character truthfully, not to indulge the character. We have to train our mind to recognize the difference. And, if I may mix my metaphors once again, we have to train our ego to feel safe letting the pilot fly the plane.

THE KEYS TO OVERRIDING THE EGO

We know that the ego feels the need to protect us. We know that the ego blocks like crazy when it feels threatened. So trying to get the ego to backoff and listen to the soul is an almost unwinnable, uphill battle, because the ego feels threatened.

We are not trying to eliminate the ego. We are just trying to bring the relationship of our human self into balance with our soul.

The way to do that is to simply recognize that everything is energy. We are all energy. Our ego is energy. We are not getting rid of the ego, we are just shifting the energy around each given issue that the ego is trying to protect us from without having to know the reason why.

In order to keep the ego from protecting us unnecessarily, there are four basic keys to keeping it in check:

Forgiveness
Letting Go
Gratitude
Love

Now I know that many of us just had our ego say, *"Yeah, right. That's lovely but… no."* Because remember: the ego is going to protect itself, because as far as the ego is concerned, it *is* us and its job is to protect us and so begins the eternal loop.

So we need to give the ego a hand with this one. We need to develop a practice that helps it relax out of its current state of protective overdrive and the belief that it has to be in control.

The four keys help override the ego and keep us in the practice of making the other player look good. And they each require us to look for the *what* instead of the *why*.

The really, really good news is that these keys to shifting the energy around the ego are all contained in one ridiculously super simple practice that we have the ancient Hawaiians to thank for.

HO'OPONOPONO

When my clients, my students, or my daughters get all wound up in a conflict with themselves or someone else, I simply tell them, "It's time to Ho'oponopono your ass off."

Ho'oponopono is an ancient Hawaiian prayer that was popularized in mainstream culture several decades ago by Dr. Ihaleakalā Hew Len, a clinical psychologist who employed Ho'oponopono in his work with patients in a large psychiatric hospital. He would say Ho'oponopono each day over the files of each client and eventually, as legend has it, the patients and the staff were all healed and transformed over time by Dr. Hew Len using Ho'oponopono.

Pono means "balance," and Ho'oponopono roughly means "moving life back into balance" or "setting things right."

Remember when the ego thinks it's flying the plane, our relationship between our two selves is out of balance. So this is that ridiculously simple practice for putting our relationship with ourselves, and therefore our life, back into balance.

Ho'oponopono is a powerful tool for refocusing energy and clearing thought habits that the ego naturally kicks into place in an attempt to protect us or find a why. It strips the why right out of the situation.

Ho'oponopono moves the ego out of the way by simply shifting the energy without needing to know the reason why it is shifting. We're just interrupting the pattern, the rut of thought and behavior that, without even realizing it, the ego gets locked into. We only need to move the ego out of the way for just a moment to let the energy have a chance to shift. We are shifting from justification, validation, vindication, and judgment to compassion and connection.

To put it in context with our metaphorical, metaphysical guide, we are accepting what is and our response-ability, letting go of attachment to outcomes, finding the gift, and finding the love.

PRACTICING HO'OPONOPONO

With Ho'oponopono, in the words of Rex, "There is no why." It is simply a mantra, a chant, or a prayer (if you will), that consists of four short phrases intended to cleanse the energy of the person saying them.

Those four phrases are:

> **I'm sorry.**
> **Please forgive me.**
> **Thank you.**
> **I love you.**

All you do when you are in conflict with anyone, with anything, or within yourself is to simply say those four phrases in succession while focusing your attention on that person, thing, situation, or whatever.

That's it. I'm not kidding.

It's energy. Energy shifts easily. We make it hard by thinking it has to be hard. But it doesn't.

Repeat those four phrases at least seven to ten times for each thing you are conflicted about and the situation will shift back toward balance. When you feel anxiety, or fear, or anger, or resentment, or feel the need to know why, just Ho'oponopono your ass off.

OK, for those of you (including me once upon a time), who feel lots of why questions coming up, let's talk about why all those whys.

WHY AM I SORRY?!

Inevitably, the minute I introduce someone who is in conflict with another player in their life to Ho'oponopono, they almost always rebel. The first phrase of Ho'oponopono is "I'm sorry" and the first thing I hear from a client or student in full blown protective personality mode is, *"Why do I have to say I'm sorry?! I don't have anything to be sorry for. I didn't do anything wrong!"*

Yeah, it's a problem. It's not a *real* problem, but the ego views it as one. Because the ego sees "Why?" as the all-important question.

The first key to uniting our two selves is forgiveness. We have to be aware of the judgment that we are holding onto. We have to understand that when we are not in forgiveness, our protective personality is saying that there are all these reasons why I should not forgive, because forgiveness makes me vulnerable. Forgiveness, like accepting, is often misunderstood as allowing, when they are both actually quite the opposite. Just as accepting is the acknowledgement of an offer that is 100% within your response-ability, so too is forgiveness. Just like accepting is acknowledging the offer, forgiveness is acknowledging the "wrong" and choosing to respond to that wrong by releasing your attachment to it and discontinuing its effect on you.

When we choose not to forgive, we are choosing to block our own freedom. Yeah, yeah, yeah. I know. We've heard it a billion times before. Forgiveness is for you, not for them, et cetera, et cetera, et cetera. It's hard to practice forgiveness. There are always going to be reasons why we feel we should stop forgiveness from happening. We can always find reasons why not to forgive if we look for them.

I also hear questions like, *"Why am I asking for forgiveness? They need to be asking me for forgiveness! This is backwards!!!"*

It's a challenge for us to let go of being right.

My dear friend Pat McDonald was a gifted songwriter and philosopher. Pat would say:

> *"You're going to have to decide, do you want to be right or do you want to be happy."*

Actually, in a lot of cases, the ego believes it is most important to be right. Being justified feels like the most important thing to that protective personality and lots of times it costs us our happiness. We get stuck in thinking about the "who's right and who's wrong" of it and we don't like the vulnerable feeling of being wrong and so we defend — otherwise known as blocking.

BLAME AND SHAME

"Why" is often looking for someone to blame or some reinforcement of shame. And if the one that we blame or the one that we shame is us, then… wow. There is no way to get away from a 24/7 cycle of blaming and shaming. The ego is trying to protect us by continuing the pattern it has established when any presets are triggered by anyone or anything, even ourselves.

If you think of the ego as a program in a game, this program has limitations. It seeks why and, since why is often about justification and validation, that leads us to punishment or retribution. If that punishment or retribution kicks in toward ourselves? Ugh. We get caught in the wheels of a really ugly cycle.

LET THE "OTHER PLAYER" BE YOU

To break the cycle of self-punishment, for just a moment, think of "I'm sorry, please forgive me, thank you, I love you" as four offers. They are four offers you are sending out into the energetic field of the cosmos. It is your ego offering to your soul the prayer of I'm sorry, please forgive me, thank you, I love you. And because your soul is you and your soul is pure source energy, we can safely assume that your soul is fully accepting that offer even if your ego is reluctant to make it.

Just saying it is all that is necessary for your soul to fully accept that energetic offering. And then it is fully returned by your soul to your egoic self. All of the forgiveness, all of the acceptance, all of the gratitude, and all of the love is accepted and returned, back and forth, on and on. Without explanation, it's just a give and take between you and you.

It will also affect others around you, as in the case of Dr. Hew Len. And really, who cares why? The bottom line is that this is a prime opportunity for you to converse between your two selves and unite them in an energetic exchange of forgiveness, letting go, gratitude, and love. It is the ultimate "Yes, and…" exercise for your two selves.

If the plane feels like it can fly itself, then why should it have to trust the pilot, let alone love them? Ho'oponopono helps the ego to fall back in love with the soul. And the more we practice it, the more natural it will become. If the ego can step into a pattern, then the energy will reconnect between the egoic self and the soul self. And that energy is pure love.

So you want to find the love? Find your connection to your soulful self. That's right, Honey. Listen to me, Honey, I'm going to *save your life*. You've got to find the love. **It's you**.

"The ego is as you think of yourself. You in relation to all the commitments of your life, as you understand them. The self is the whole range of possibilities that you've never even thought of. And you're stuck with your past when you're stuck with the ego. Because if all you know about yourself is what you found out about yourself, well, that already happened. The self is a whole field of potentialities to come through."

- Joseph Campbell

CHAPTER 9
PLAYING THE LEAD

"There is a vitality, a life force, a quickening that is translated through you into action, and because there is only one of you in all time, this expression is unique. And if you block it, it will never exist through any other medium and be lost."

\- **Martha Graham**

NOTHING CAPRICIOUS HERE

"There's nothing capricious in nature, and the implanting of a desire indicates that its gratification is in the constitution of the creature that feels it."

-   Ralph Waldo Emerson

In this production on the great stage of life, we came here for a reason. We came to play a role and experience the growth process of moving toward our bliss. We were cast in this role, within this particular production, quite intentionally and quite specifically.

And what's more, you are perfectly cast in this role. How do you know? You are here. You are you. You are the only *you* there is. So, yeah. You are the perfect you.

Our character has a purpose, and we are here to recognize that purpose, understand it, and fulfill it to the best of our ability. That's the journey we are on, the story we are in, the game we are playing — pick a metaphor, it all works.

We are here *on purpose,* as in intentionally (something we intended to do).

And!

We are here *on purpose,* as in on track or in alignment with our sacred purpose (what we came to be, do, and share).

But when we lose our belief in that, that's when we get off track.

REMEMBER THE FISHIES

You remember my second favorite metaphor from our friend Mr. Einstein:

"If you ask a fish to climb a tree..."

Everyone is brilliant. Everyone is a genius, at something, at *their* thing. But if the expectation is that they are to be a genius at a *particular* thing, they run the risk of spending their life wasted, feeling stupid and inadequate. In other words, everyone is perfectly cast in the role they came here to play.

That means that if we came here as a fish, or a giraffe, or a platypus, or a lion, we did it **on purpose**.

Our being a fish is not a mistake; it's what we meant to do.

The first thing we have to accept in this giant improv of life is who we are. We have to accept the character that we are playing unconditionally. Our job here on this stage is to be the best us we can be. That's not a cliché. That's a fact.

You can't lose the real you. You can hide it, you can block it, you can see it as an obstacle, but the truth is, it's only an obstacle to the well-meaning monkeys.

If you are a lion, that is really, really cool. But again, society is not expecting lions. They're expecting monkeys. So the monkeys, however well-meaning, get disappointed, embarrassed, and frustrated when you act like a lion. And then they get seriously engaged in the process of fixing you.

You're a lion. That's just fine. And even if every day up until this one you have been trying to stuff every inch of your wonderful lion-ness into an ill-fitting, suffocating monkey suit in an effort to fit in, never fear. No matter how long you have spent in that monkey suit, no matter how much it has pinched and itched, inside you are still 110% the beautiful lion that is you.

> *It's not that you don't fit the suit,*
> *it's that the suit doesn't fit you.*

The most important thing is to honor who you naturally are. You were born perfectly enabled with all these natural gifts. You were born perfectly enabled with "much."

EMBRACING MUCH

I have a client/student, Mabel, who felt out of place on a daily basis and had people constantly telling her she was "too much." She was already familiar with my metaphorical monkey story. So I'm going to tell you exactly what I told her.

Of course you are too much. You are a lion. You were born perfectly enabled with all of these wonderful talents. You were born with "much." Much is a gift. It is not a problem. It's only a problem for the monkeys because they think you ought to be focused on climbing the tree, not on roaring. But you are this gorgeous lion who is glorious at roaring. Relax into that rather than worrying about how "much" plays in a field of monkeys. Realize that, even if you are the only lion on the planet, that doesn't mean you are the worst at being a monkey.

It means there is no one else on the planet who is better at being a lion than you.

If you are "much," much is what you meant to be.

Much is not a problem. It's only a problem for the monkeys.

You function very well with the monkeys. You do all the things that the monkeys do. You stand on your back legs and you figure out how to use your lion claws to climb the tree. You might be able to be a passable monkey, even an above average monkey, but you are already an absolutely perfect lion.

The only reason the monkeys think you are too much is because the reality is that you could eat them for dinner.

So of course they want you to be quiet. You belong on the ground. You can get in that tree and you can pretend all you want, but you are never going to feel your best imitating a monkey. So, stop it! Stop pretending to be a monkey. Stop explaining the fact that you are not a monkey. Stop making excuses for why you can't do monkey things.

Be a lion.

> *"Overcome the notion that we must be regular;*
> *it robs you of the chance to be extraordinary."*

> - Uta Hagen

ACCEPTING THE ROLE

Accepting your role is about honoring who you naturally are. You are the only you. You are never going to get better at being you by trying to be more like someone else. If you are not fitting in, it is not that there is something wrong with you, it means that place does not fit you.

What you were born with in your heart is who you are. The rest is that critic telling you what's right or wrong from the monkey point of view.

In acting as in life, acting as if it is true is how we make it true. The goal is to think, decide, and act as the you that you mean to be.

ACTORS ARE THE EXPERT ON THAT ROLE

Lots of times, young inexperienced actors think their job is to come into a role and do whatever the director tells them to do. The first reframing that is necessary is to teach them that *they* are the expert on their role. They are the expert on that character.

Only you know what your calling is. Only you know what your purpose and passion is. It does not matter that you are the best by someone else's standards. In the words of my youngest daughter Brittni:

"I may never be the best photographer in the world, but there is no other photographer like me."

Knowing who you are and knowing what you are called to do is the first step to accepting the role.

THE CONTENT OF YOUR CHARACTER

When an actor comes into a role, even before they arrive at rehearsal, they dive into the role through diligent work in text and character analysis. They do their research to learn as much from the text as they can in order to inform their decisions about behavior and choices that are true to the character based on that text.

Well, in life, we don't have a text to analyze. We don't see the script ahead of time and so that's not the source of our research. So where do we look to find our clues? What do we research in order to discover the truth behind our choices and behaviors?

LOOKING AT THE ANCIENT TEXT

When we are unsure of how to move forward, it is human nature to look back to those who came before us to help us decide what action we should take or what choice we should make. The challenge is that no matter how similar the question being addressed in that ancient text, it cannot ever be the same question because the lions, fish, and monkeys of that time were living in a completely different forest. Yet we look at ancient texts that someone wrote ten, one-hundred, or one-thousand years ago and we assume that they are writing the instructions for how to live our life right now.

For those of you who are gamers, that's like thinking the way to learn to play a game that came out today is to go get the instruction booklet for Pong from 1972. That seems silly when we put it that way, but Pong has as much in common with video games today as the picture of life thousands of years ago in Babylonia or Mesopotamia has with life today in New York, Paris, or Moscow.

THE ANSWER IS

Here's the real kicker: many of us, including me, spend a lot of time reading ancient texts or reading/listening to current "thought leaders" interpret what someone else has written down a thousand years ago. And guess what. You know what they are all saying? The answer is within. At the end of the day, that's all they say. The answer is written within you, in your heart, from your soul.

The answer is you.

You, the player, has to research the character which is also YOU!!! And that research does not reside outside you. You have to go within.

DEFAULTING TO SOMEONE ELSE'S TEXT

Many of us want to default to someone else's text. We feel safe following rules that someone else wrote down, so we base our character analysis on what someone else thinks it should be. But that is the mistake that leads to us trying to be "like" someone else. That creates a false performance.

When an actor sets out to do research on their character, they don't go ask the other actors what they think their character is like. It is their job to show up on the first day of rehearsal as the expert on their own character. They're not coming to be handed whatever the director or anyone else tells them; they show up with their goals and objectives already developed.

When you sit down to play a game, do you go ask everyone else you know who has played it before which character you should play and how you can get through to the end? No! Why not? 'Cause all the fun would go bye-bye! We don't want to know how someone else did it. We wanna do it!

When an actor approaches a role, the worst thing they can do is watch someone else's performance of the same role. Then they are setting a goal of imitation and comparison rather than one of discovery and creation. Centuries after it was first performed, people still flock to see Hamlet. While the story itself is part of it, the real reason is they want to see those actors give their unique take on something they have seen time and again. The value is in that person's performance, one that can be done by no one else.

On this stage of life, we are often reluctant to play our role full out unless we've seen someone else play a version of it first. No matter how many people you can find who have lived a life similar to yours or done the things you love to do before you, you did not come here to redo what they did. They discovered their own way of doing it and so will you, if you trust the inner guidance that comes from your soul.

THE TEXT WITHIN

We have a treasure trove of information within us on the character we are playing. Now, you might think that you came in as a blank slate, but no. You didn't. That's just a convenient excuse to opt out of the responsibility of doing the work to discover your unique purpose.

You came here with what many may argue is the "nature" part of "nature vs nurture." In other words, you came here with a whole bunch of likes, dislikes, propensities, and tendencies. Recognizing and honoring those things is the first place to start when researching your character.

You have passions and dreams and likes and dislikes for a reason. The combination of them makes up the you that you came here to be. Sometimes those deep inner values have been buried under piles of judgements that we acquired from ourselves, our family, and our society. But the good news is that we are connected in every moment to the original text of our journey on this planet. We have access within ourselves to the ultimate well from which our dreams and desires spring.

QUESTIONING THE CHARACTER

When seeking out the information that will lead us to our sacred purpose, all we have to do is trust the text within. We have to ask ourselves the questions that we would ask of a character.

"What do I want or need most in life?"

- In acting, we call this a super-objective. It's the overarching objective that spans the entire story.

"What do I want or need most in this situation or circumstance?"

- In acting, we call this the objective. It is situational and changes from circumstance to circumstance.

"What do I have to do, step by step, to go after what I need?"

- In acting, we call these actions or tactics. They're the moment-to-moment specific choices that you make to go about getting what you want.

"What are the obstacles in the way of what I want or need?"

- Even though we understand what obstacles are, we need to go through the process of reframing them. How can I embrace the obstacles? What is the gift in that obstacle?

Just as our performance in a play is better when we have a clear intention, so too is our performance in life when we behave from a place of understanding what we truly want (our objective). Then we focus our intention, clearly and precisely, and take exact steps (actions) to affect the world around us. And, finally, we behave from a place of honesty, meaning that if we behave as if it is true, we will arrive at our destination. If we do these things, we will have had a fully committed, positive performance.

DOING YOUR TEXT AND CHARACTER ANALYSIS

Once an actor accepts a role, the first thing they do is character development and text analysis to inform the choices that they are about to make in order to play the character as authentically as possible.

They don't just go into the role with a one-size-fits-all approach—not if they are going to be successful at portraying fully-formed human beings. They determine the values, wants, dreams, and desires of this character (objectives) and then go about determining the strategies or tactics with which they are going to pursue them (actions).

An actor doing their job will often do a much deeper dive into the inner workings of a character they are going to play than most of us do on ourselves in our actual lives.

So if we give that same amount of intention to the role we are playing as *us* in *this* life, we need to investigate what makes us tick. What is it that we truly want? What is it that we have been lastingly affected by in our lives and how do we want to deal with that?

YOU'RE BORN TO PLAY THIS ROLE

Every actor cast in a particular role is cast because of the inherent qualities, talents, characteristics, and abilities that they come in with. That's intentional. If someone has to sword fight, dance, or sing in their role, a director does not cast someone with no ability to do that. Actors come into the role with the essential abilities already there, they just have to apply them in this particular context.

The same is true for us in life. When exploring the character of us, we have to begin by fundamentally accepting that who we are, all of our natural talents, propensities, and qualities, are exactly what we meant to have in order to give our best performance in this particular role, at this particular time, in this particular production.

FINDING YOUR BLISS

"If you do follow your bliss you put yourself on a kind of track that has been there all the while, waiting for you, and the life that you ought to be living is the one you are living."

\- Joseph Campbell

Finding your bliss is finding the love on steroids. What Mario meant was: find what the character loves and that will help you understand what you need to be pursuing on their behalf. When you find the love of a character, you find their authenticity.

In order for an actor to authentically play a character, they must know what the character loves. In order for you to authentically show up as yourself in your life, you must know what *you* love.

As strange as it may sound, we can't take for granted that we know our deepest passion, our deepest love, because odds are we have never spent time exploring it with ourselves. In fact, most of us put a lot of energy into explaining to ourselves why we can't have what we love, why we won't pursue our passion, or why we can't or shouldn't want our dream.

What do you love? In order to fully show up on this planet we must fully embrace the love at the center of our being, and work to express it in the most authentic way possible.

"Everybody has a calling.
Your real job in life is to figure out why you are here
and get about the business of doing it."

\- Oprah Winfrey

DIVINE DISCONTENT

It's that calling felt deep within. It's like a voice inside that says good enough is not good enough. That feeling is what some call divine discontent. Divine discontent is a feeling given to you (personality) by you (soul). It comes from that part of you that knows, full well, what you were born for and what you were meant to do. It is whispering to you, sometimes softly and sometimes quite intensely, but always from a beautiful place of love and divine inspiration.

It's calling to you to find the love *in you*.

If you listen to the whisper of divine discontent and take it as an offer, accept it, and offer back, it will save you from that black hole of fear that leads us right to boring.

Because, again, the Universe only offers, and it is not offering us the opportunity for pain, frustration, and boredom. Those feelings come from blocking and only we can do that.

SHARING A SECRET

I'll tell you a little secret about me. I have had many people over the years tell me that they think of me as fearless. The first several times that someone said that to me, if I happened to be drinking something, it elicited an indelicate spit-take. If I wasn't drinking, I would just out and out chuckle. They had to be joking. That was the opposite of how I saw myself.

I was pretty much terrified *all the time*.

I was afraid of going to NYC to pursue an acting career in a city where I knew no one with a dream that people scoffed at.

I was afraid of going to London to study at the National Theatre when umm… I wasn't the most financially sound.

I was afraid when I was packing up a four-year-old and everything we owned to go across the country to accept a fellowship in a city we had never been to, especially since we didn't even have an apartment to live in.

I was afraid of starting a professional theater company.

I was afraid of directing controversial plays.

I was afraid of starting theater programs for at-risk youth.

And on, and on, and on…

I was never fearless, I was very, very scared.

But, through all of it, the fear that was greater than the fear of doing it was the fear of never trying. Sure, I knew that I could bomb, but worse than the fear of bombing was the dread of getting to the end of my life and wishing I had tried. There is nothing more yucky to me than the idea of regret. It's that feeling that if you don't pursue it (whatever it is), you will get to the end of your life with nothing but questions of what could have been.

That, to me, makes everything else seem far less dangerous.

THE PAIN OF NOT

My favorite quote from the Gospel of Thomas is #70 where Jesus says:

"If you bring forth what is within you, what you bring forth will save you. If you do not bring forth what is within you, what you do not bring forth will destroy you."

It sounds intense, I know, but sometimes the truth is intense.

This quote is telling us, in no uncertain terms, that if we offer what we were born to bring to this planet, then it will save us (bring us bliss). If we do not do it, that will destroy us (give us a life of frustration and pain).

Or, to put it another way, if you bring forth what you were meant to on this planet, you will discover heaven on earth. If you don't, you'll discover hell on earth.

Heaven is living your bliss; hell is the pain of not.

When people wonder why they are miserable when they've got plenty of money, plenty of stuff, and plenty of other outward signs of success or happiness, it's because they never honored their unique creative genius, their purpose, or their passion. All of that was inside them, but they didn't do it. They didn't express it because of all the practical reasons. They didn't do it and now there's a hole inside them. There's a deficit, a problem, and they can't figure out what it is, but it's because their passion was never honored.

I promise you that whatever your passion and your purpose, whatever that feeling deep inside that is nudging you toward something greater, it was not given to you to cause you pain or frustration by not getting it. That love, that desire, that talent, that calling is there to inspire you, not to frustrate you.

The frustration comes from not pursuing it.

Now you might think that if it's truly your purpose, pursuing it should be easy. But remember, overcoming the obstacles is part of the process.

People give up on their passion and purpose all the time because they run into an obstacle and then interpret that as the Universe or some other force beyond themselves telling them no. But since we know that the Universe never blocks, that's when we have to remember that those obstacles are happening for us and not to us.

"Bring into play the almighty power within you,
so that on the stage of life you can fulfill
your high destined role."

- Paramahansa Yogananda

THE GOLDEN BUDDHA

You have possibly heard the legend of the Golden Buddha. It has taken on many variations in the telling and retelling, but the essential story is that of a statue of a golden Buddha.

For nearly 200 years, the Buddha was covered in a layer of stucco to prevent it from being looted or destroyed by hostile invaders. Eventually, there came a time when no one remembered that the Buddha was actually made of gold. The Buddha had been assumed to be just a stone Buddha, precious as an instrument of worship but not priceless, unique, and extraordinary in its very makeup.

Then one day, quite by accident, a chunk of the stucco broke off.

That is what allowed the gold to show through and the joyful process of uncovering the Buddha began.

The Golden Buddha is a real, actual statue. It's right there in the temple of Wat Traimit, Bangkok, Thailand, publicly displayed along with pieces of the stucco that used to cover it. It's just the story of how the gold started to show through that gets changed in various retellings. The story is a beautiful one about covering this sacred, golden statue with a stone shell in order to protect it and then forgetting what it truly is inside. And then the crisis happens: it gets dropped or bumped and a little chunk of that outer shell drops off to reveal the true nature of the Buddha within.

The metaphor of the Golden Buddha is (yes, I know, it's another one, but come on! This is a metaphorical, metaphysical guide, so what did you expect?) a metaphor for ourselves.

We are that Golden Buddha. When we see danger coming, the protective personality covers us up in our hard, protective shell. Over time, we forget that we were ever gold.

We forget what is under that protective shell and we see and treat ourselves as the stone shell makes us seem.

Until…

CRACKING THE CHRYSALIS

In a recent coaching session with my client Gigi (who was a master blocker, by the way), she reached a revelation about the impact of doing this kind of work, which she had once dismissed as trivial because it was based in acting and improvisation. Over a zoom call one morning, she shouted at me, *"Oh my god! I thought this stuff was just playing, just fun, not an instrument for cracking open the chrysalis of your life!"*

I love that phrase. Cracking open the chrysalis of our lives indeed. It's breaking the stone shell that is hiding the Golden Buddha within.

We are the player, the character, and the treasure that we are seeking at the end of the story — it's all us.

The *true* us.

SCARY STUFF

But we get scared. We are scared to take that shell off because it was put there to protect us by our beautiful, perhaps hyperactive, protective personality.

As Richard Bach says in his novel *Illusions*:

> *"What the caterpillar calls the end of the world, the master calls a butterfly."*

The point where we become the butterfly is the point at which we are aware of ourselves as the player, the soul, the Golden Buddha — not limited at all by the shell or the perception of our limitations that we have learned after we arrived on this planet.

CHAPTER 10
SHARING THE STAGE

*"One's performance is often heightened
by the brilliance and generosity
of other actors."*

\-   **Cyril Cusack**

THEATER IS A COLLABORATIVE ART FORM

And so is life.

Meaning, in short, you can't do this alone.

In the theater, there is no such thing as a truly solo performance. There is no performance on any stage where the performer has no help whatsoever from another person. Even a one-person show on a bare stage has someone to turn the lights on and off.

You're on a team. It's *your* team. You cast them. Everyone playing the supporting roles, everyone turning a light on, everyone handing you a prop—they are all there *for you*. Even the antagonists. They are all offers. They are all *making* offers. They may be blocking, but even that is an offer.

> *"Every individual matters.*
> *Every individual has a role to play.*
> *Every individual makes a difference."*

> \- Jane Goodall

Let's just roll with the Jane Goodall theme here for a moment.

DISCOVERING WHO YOU SHARE THE PLANET WITH

When scientists discover a new creature on earth, they don't immediately judge it for what it doesn't do. They observe it to find out what it *does* and what comes naturally to it.

Imagine what would happen if we treated each new person we met in the same way. What if we recognized that judging the brilliance of every person on the planet based on one specific set of criteria, created by and for people with a specific set of aptitudes, attitudes, needs, and expectations, is as crazy as judging every animal on the planet based on its ability to climb a tree? Because it is.

The systems in society (groups of well-meaning monkeys), tend to hold tight to those judgements of aptitudes, talents, and intelligence that they have set up themselves or been trained to believe. The way we tend to respond to that systemic set of judgements, when we become consciously aware and frustrated by them, is to want to change the system.

We fight the system and build up all the ammunition that we rely on to state our case so that we can get the system to change.

But what we don't do is change *us*. We change, yes, but not intentionally and not for the better. The change is far too often a change to feeling helpless and hopeless against the system and, worse yet, we unconsciously buy into the systems' judgements.

Perhaps we don't buy into them for ourselves (our inner fish), and perhaps we rail against them on behalf of our loved ones (the wonderful giraffes and lions in our lives), but we inadvertently join with the system in terms of judging the various aardvarks, platypuses, and pangolins we come across in our daily lives

So, after the deep dive into changing the way we look at our own performance in this role of a lifetime, it's now time to look at the way we can change how we approach the other members of our ensemble.

"Be the change you want to see in the world."

\- Mahatma Gandhi

BE THE CHANGE

Remember that the fundamental premise of this book (and all my work really), is that each and every human on this planet is a unique creative genius—you included.

But not just you, *EVERYONE!*

See, the thing is, with as much time as we've spent discussing how brilliant you are and how to share that brilliance, we've spent relatively little time addressing the fact that, just as you are a brilliant, unique creative genius, *SO IS EVERYONE ELSE.*

Just as we have been learning to consider our own thoughts, feelings, ideas, imaginings, and passions as not just good or bad, but important, worthwhile, valuable, and bursting with potential, we must also learn that *SO ARE EVERYONE ELSE'S!*

We can't just go on our merry way expecting the system to magically change. We can't just expect to wake up in a new world where everyone will be able to respect the genius of all the other players on the planet. We can't just wait.

We have to *create* the change. We have to *be* the change. We have to change the way we see and treat *all* of our fellow players.

"If we could change ourselves, the tendencies in the world would also change. As a man changes his own nature, so does the attitude of the world change towards him. This is the divine mystery supreme. A wonderful thing it is and the source of our happiness. We need not wait to see what others do."

- Mahatma Gandhi

MISSING THE POINT

Several years ago, my dear friend Carla and I traveled to Salt Lake City for a seminar with a deeply respected thought leader who I am going to refer to as John. John is a *New York Times* bestselling author many times over and a major force in New Thought and Self-Help circles. At this seminar, he said to a room of more than 1,000 people:

"Everyone is brilliant."

Carla was bouncing up and down in her chair. With a huge smile, she hit my leg and whisper-screamed, *"He's saying your thing!"*

"Everyone is a genius in their own way," John continued, *"and I mean everyone."*

At this point, Carla was effervescent. She was tapping my leg and my arm and bouncing with so much excitement because his perspective was exactly like mine! I was grinning just as big as she was because I felt beyond validated. My grounding philosophy was being affirmed in a huge way.

And then John said, *"Well, maybe not everyone. Maybe not someone with Down Syndrome, but almost everyone."*

You know in a movie, when an explosion happens and all the main character can hear is a high-pitched ringing? Yeah, it was like that. I was not only shellshocked, I was nauseated, disgusted, and outright offended. But more than that, I was completely heartbroken. After all these years, I thought I recognized the monkeys and could see them coming.

It was life-altering, because John was one of the most well-meaning monkeys of them all. ***He just didn't get it***. He was looking down from the top of the tree and writing off the fish as if he knew, for a fact, that they were never going to be able to climb it.

He mistook feeling sorry for the fish as compassion, when in reality he was too narrow-minded to realize that the fish would find their own way.

So let me be abundantly clear. When I say everyone is brilliant, *I MEAN **EVERYONE***. Everyone, regardless of age, education, or perceived ability, is a unique creative genius. And for those that came to this planet with challenges and obstacles in the way of them sharing that genius, then it's on the rest of us to show up with the compassion, curiosity, and respect that gives them the opportunity to share that genius.

EXPECTING AND ACCEPTING
EVERYTHING AS BRILLIANT

We know that expectations are presets. We also know that I am very fond of saying things like, "Expectation is the death of spontaneity," or, "Expectation is where spontaneous thoughts go to die." And that's all true. But that type of expectation refers to an attachment to a particular outcome or limiting belief.

But I'll tell you something else that's true.

Positive expectation—curiosity coupled with a belief in unlimited possibility and faith in the brilliance of another—is *magic* in the making.

I learned about what happens when you expect brilliance when I noticed something that was happening in my classes. It goes back to that comment I mentioned earlier that was made about my teaching style:

"You know what I love about Ms. Cavanaugh?
She teaches like she doesn't know there is anything
you can't do… and so there isn't."

I was in a classroom where every day, several times a day, I told this room full of students with debilitating special needs that they were brilliant. They were, but no one had ever called them that before. The more I said it and the more I treated them that way, the more they came to offer their brilliance without hesitation.

I walked into this classroom day after day where the kids supposedly "couldn't do" whatever I was about to ask them to do, only to find that they did it and more. They surprised their teachers, they surprised their support staff, they surprised their families, and they even surprised themselves.

That is where I came to understand that respect and compassion exponentially expands creativity and the expression of creative genius.

My expectation for myself as a teacher, a director, a coach, a parent, and a human is always that it is my responsibility to find the brilliance in each and every human I encounter.

THE POINT

In the mid 2010's, I was doing a residency in a special education class teaching high school students with disabilities, most of whom were believed to be unable to write three coherent sentences, and some of whom were nearly or entirely non-verbal. They had conditions ranging from mosaic down syndrome to autism and seizure disorders.

One young man, who I will call Peter, had become my favorite for a multitude of reasons, not the least of which was because he was an amazing master blocker.

Peter had a seizure disorder which made speaking very difficult for him. Because his speech was so halted, people assumed him to not have many cohesive thoughts. But I quickly realized in working with him that he had quite an active mind behind the difficult and stilted means of expression that masked his brilliance.

After meeting with these students, I decided (in my absolutely spontaneous way) that I wanted to teach them to write stories that were far beyond anything they had ever done before. So I taught them improvisation skills. I taught them how to imagine characters. I taught them the elements of a story and how there is always a beginning, a middle, and an end.

A lot of the students couldn't write for themselves, or at least they couldn't write fast enough to keep up with their incredible thought processes. Since the very act of writing created a struggle that didn't need to be there, I brought scribes into the classroom on a regular basis. These scribes were either volunteer students or trained special education assistants. The young volunteers always inevitably ended up being better scribes because they were less inclined to try and "help" the students as much as the trained workers were.

See, adults with training were more likely to make suggestions than listen which, in Peter's case especially, was a recipe for disaster.

I posed questions to the class to help further their thinking. What was their central character's height and body type? What did their character eat for breakfast that morning? What were their likes and dislikes? The students would talk and the scribes would write. But Peter often took lengthy periods before he would speak. He would stare off into space and people would not only assume that he was not intending to answer the question, but that he had no thoughts on the matter at all.

The scribes Peter worked with were very well-meaning monkeys. They thought they were being super extra helpful by making as many suggestions as they could because they assumed that it was more important to get a bunch of stuff written down than it was to give Peter the opportunity for expression.

Once again, enter my teaching toddler. Shelly, who was now in her mid-20's, had grown up working alongside me in all sorts of situations. She just gets it. So when I could not find a suitable scribe for Peter among those trained to "help," I brought Shelly into the classroom.

Shelly knew the situation she was walking into. She knew that no matter how long he took, she was to just sit there, wait, and then write down exactly what he said. So that's what she did and admittedly, after the first day, it looked as though he had not understood my questions, and the story he was writing seemed to make very little sense. However, Shelly returned day after day and sat beside Peter, waiting patiently and writing down each word he said verbatim.

After several days, a miracle unveiled itself. Peter's seemingly nonsensical story had become a seven-page, post-apocalyptic tale of a young boy in a tent city. It was a moving, cohesive, surrealist tale that seemed lightyears beyond the capabilities of what most people expected from Peter or any of his classmates.

So here's the point. And it's so important that if you only take a handful of things away from this book, I want this to be one of them.

We don't know exactly what form the brilliance will take in each of our fellow players, but we must believe that it is there.

CHANGING THE WORLD

Suppose that we walk into every room knowing that everyone we see is brilliant at something, at *their* thing, in their way. And suppose that we presume it to be part of our job as another human sharing the planet with them to discover what that brilliance is.

You see, I'm not suggesting that we leave that response-ability to the teachers, family members, colleagues, or caregivers. I'm talking about everyone. We must treat everyone in this production as a vital member of our cast and crew.

Believe me, if they are in your life, in your scene, they are valuable. Whether they have one line or 2,000, they are important to the story in that moment.

Peter changed my life. He changed Shelly's life. He taught us about patience and perseverance and that sometimes the reason a person is blocking is simply because they are trying to defend themselves from the pain of having been blocked at every turn for years on end.

We have to assume brilliance. It's the key to the most successful experience here. We must assume that all our fellow players are brilliant and perfectly cast in their own role with a passion and a purpose to their life as profound as any that we might discover for ourselves.

In order to share the great stage of life with compassion and clarity, we must see our fellow players through a prism of possibility, rather than a prism of limitation. We do that by eliminating some of the limiting beliefs that prevent us from opening up to the field of infinite possibility waiting inside every incarnated soul.

THE C-WORDS

Comparison, Conformity, Compromise, and Competition—these four common C-words actually comprise a dangerous cluster of misleading concepts. All four of these C-words are products of Monkey philosophy that we have come to look at as not only positive, but something we should strive for. The insidious danger lies in the fact that, even worse than their individual direct effects, they collectively drown out and minimize the importance of three of the best C-words in the English language: Cooperation, Compassion, and yes, Creativity.

I realize that you may believe that at least a few of these words on my dangerous list are good. It is also equally likely that you do not see any of them as actually bad or dangerous. But within the metaphorical metaphysical journey we are embarking on, they indeed are, for they lead to judgment and fear.

In the theater, the concepts of Comparison, Conformity, Compromise, and Competition are painful and dangerous. In life, they are literally designed to counteract the free and unrestricted flow of each individual's unique creative genius. So let's get their misunderstandings out of the way.

COMPARISON

It's a terribly shortsighted actor who wants to be on stage with people less talented than themselves. Just ask any massively talented actor in a Broadway show that closed on the first night. Life, like theater, is collaborative and neither of those collaborations are enhanced by comparison. Comparison is far more likely to diminish the collaboration as well as the expression of the individual.

Let's look at the Miriam-Webster definition of comparison just for a sec:

- an examination of two or more items to establish similarities and dissimilarities

Comparison can be useful when choosing a car or picking a piece of fruit, but comparison of ourselves or our performance to another requires us to choose either ourselves or the other person as being less than in some way. Yeah, how about not. Remember that part of our journey is to learn to expect and respect the unique creative genius in ourselves and all those around us, not to decide which one of us has more or less than the other.

No genius is better than another's because, say it with me, *each genius is unique.*

Once more to Miriam-Webster, unique is defined as:

- being the only one : SOLE
- being without a like or equal : UNEQUALED
- distinctively characteristic : PECULIAR
- able to be distinguished from all others of its class or type : DISTINCT

Unequaled. Sole. Peculiar. Distinct. Why would we want to be anything else? And I'm asking "why" intentionally here, so: *Why?!* What is the benefit to the protective personality to compare?

IN ANSWER TO THE WHY

Another C-word that comes to mind here is camouflage. How do we hide from enemy fire? Camouflage. We don't stand out and we don't show ourselves to be out of the ordinary. We stay cautious (which also happens to start with C) and blend in. It's safer. But there's just one problem — *it's not what we came here to do!*

Nobody intentionally steps on a stage *not* to be seen! And I've got news for all of us: we are here intentionally! Why hide? Why blend in? Why camouflage? Why compare? It's the work of the protective personality. Fitting in and masking our greatness is a way we make ourselves feel safe.

The real antidote to comparison is empowerment.

The more that we honor, explore, and enjoy the unique wonder of each and every human being on the planet, the less comparison will even occur to us. The more we focus on empowering others, the less we will compare them or ourselves to anyone else in a negative context.

There is nothing to compare yourself to. There is no one else who is comparable to you. You were cast in this role because nobody else on the planet is better at playing you than you are. And the answer to what will make a better you is on the inside, not on the outside.

CONFORMITY

OK. I don't even think I need to say it at this point, but this is definitely, absolutely, categorically *not* what we are here for! But you already knew that.

Conforming results from having been compared to the norm and having been found lacking in some way. Conformity is a *very* monkey-oriented concept. You are either too much or too little. You are either a lion with too much roar or a fish with too little ability to climb the tree. In either case, those well-meaning monkeys trying to help you fit in will ask you politely, or perhaps not so politely, to learn to show up in the *right* way. And of course, the right way is almost always the way that is the most convenient and most familiar to the monkeys.

Conforming means finding the norm and joining it. It means establishing, defining, and continuing the processes and practices that have gone before. It does not mean creativity. It does not mean free-flowing offers. It does not mean the expression of each individual's unique creative genius. It means deciding what genius looks like and only accepting those offers that fit that model.

Basically, conforming is the anti-spontaneous brilliance version of life.

Conforming is often confused with maturing. But a mature actor is *more* able to express themselves, not less. Maturing should not result in less creativity.

Let me repeat that for emphasis:

Maturing should not result in less creativity.

Maturing should result in an ever-expanding range of creative expression. But sadly, when people mistake conforming for maturity, they become someone who does not rock the boat, does not question, does not take risks, and does not contribute anything new. When we conform, we are actually sacrificing our unique creative genius on the altar of the norm.

COMPROMISE

I'm guessing that compromise probably seems too good to be on the dangerous word list. I mean, we're taught pretty much from birth that compromise is the way to solve conflict of any kind. We're told that healthy relationships are about compromise. And pardon my apparent blocking, but no. No, they are not.

We already know what relationships are about. Healthy relationships are about healthy status interactions. It's about making the other player look good. It's about compassion, collaboration, improvisation, and being totally present with the other player. It's about listening. It's about offering, accepting, and not blocking. And, most importantly, it's about finding the love!

Compromise is, by definition, a situation where conflict is resolved by each side giving up something in order to move forward. We've been taught that there is nobility in sacrificing something in the name of compromise. But what if that something we gave up was an important piece of us? We are left feeling frustrated and disempowered because compromise is actually a mutually agreed upon form of blocking.

Compromise rarely causes harmony; it just ceases open hostility. But the underlying frustration remains because the offering and accepting process is necessarily curtailed.

Compassion and cooperation are the true paths to creative solutions that don't cause anyone frustration or pain because of what they gave up.

AND FOR THE RECORD

Conflict is not on the bad C-word list because it's not bad. It is necessary for inspiration. We confuse aggression or hostility with conflict. But in truth, two conflicting things cause us to think about how to bring them into harmony. That's what inspires us toward creative solutions.

If we deal with conflict as an invitation to offer and accept until a solution is discovered, rather than block until a compromise is reached, we will have far more true harmony in our relationships and in the world.

AND FINALLY, COMPETITION

There is a mythology that has existed throughout modern humanity that suggests we are in competition for everything. The myth has been propagated that nature is based on competition like how we've come to view the phrase "survival of the fittest."

There is nothing natural about competition.

Competition is not the fundamental rule of nature—cooperation is. We know this because all the world's a stage and the fastest way to destroy a production is to have the players competing with one another. A successful production on the stage and on the great stage of life requires cooperation of all the players involved.

Competition is structured blocking. In competition, someone is winning and someone is losing. The "winner" is blocking the "loser" from getting to the goal.

Competition comes from a deep-seated practice of comparison and a deep-seated belief in lack. Competition is taught to us as though it is a rule of survival. It is not. It is a rule of ego survival. It is an overreaction to feeling like there is not enough for everyone. But let me remind you that life is not a zero-sum game.

WHAT ARE WE HERE FOR?

You're not here to compete. You are here to share.

You are not here to compare yourself to others, but to learn to value and nurture the brilliance in yourself and all those around you.

You are not here to compromise your genius, but to collaborate and cooperate with the genius of others.

And you are certainly not here to conform! You are here to shine along with every other human on the planet.

We are all here to share our ideas and inspirations joyfully and playfully and to share the world stage gracefully and peacefully with one another.

Share, nurture, and shine! That's what it's all about.

Repeat it with me:

If it is true for any of us, it is possible for all of us, or else it isn't true at all.

That's the mantra that I want you to repeat every single time you start to doubt yourself or anyone else.

THE NON-EXISTENT CRITIC

"More than in any other performing arts the lack of respect for acting seems to spring from the fact that every layman considers himself a valid critic."

- Uta Hagen

On opening night of any production, there is one member of the audience that is perceived as having a great deal more power in that moment than any other. That person is the critic. In the theater, a critic is often feared. Their opinion, in the form of a positive or negative review, is capable of either filling or emptying the seats of your theater. They can demoralize once excited actors, end a director's career, and destroy a playwright's opportunity to share their story with the world. And anecdotally, the critic often has no prerequisite skill in the theater themselves. They may not even have a great deal of experience as a writer. They have an opinion, as does everyone else. The thing that distinguishes their opinion is that it gets a megaphone.

The opening night of a play is an event, and so we know when the critique, good or bad, is going to occur.

But on the great stage of life, every day is another showing, which means another opportunity for a negative review to be posted on the bulletin board of our brain.

And the trouble with that is the critic in our lives has just as much power to demoralize our performance or even shut down our entire production as the professional theater critic, but only if we let them.

We have mentors that we revere and critics that we fear and the trouble is that we hear the critics' voices repeated in our heads far more than the mentors'. Negative reviews have far more impact than neutral ones and arguably more impact than positive ones.

Even the critics in our lives who we haven't seen in years can still haunt our inspiration to this day. Think about that for a second and let it sink in. The bully that told you that you were stupid to wear those shoes or eat that food or write that story or sing that song? That person is running your life right now, if you let them. They are dictating what you do and do not feel comfortable doing today. They have defined your sense of "not good enough."

They may have been cruel, or they may have simply been a well-meaning monkey, letting you know that your monkey suit was falling off. Either way, they are old news. They are not talking to you, they are talking to a you of the past that no longer exists.

Just as with the theater critic, our life critic may not have any skill, wisdom, or experience that makes their opinion more valid than our own. But unlike the theater critic, they have no megaphone to amplify their opinion unless we give it to them. Don't. Just because someone shares their opinion with you does not mean that you have to give that offer the power to block you or lower your status in any way.

WE ARE "THEY"

It's important to remember that we are part of the "they" that others are worried about. When we worry about what "they" will think, do think, or might think, it is essential that we remember that, for other people, *we are they*. Especially if we are in a leadership position or a position of high status.

You may not think this applies to you because you don't think of yourself as being in a high-status position. But you need to remember that, depending on the situation, if you are a parent, teacher, mechanic, bank teller, waiter, sibling, janitor, friend, salesclerk, line cook, proctologist, or tour guide, your status can be very, very high.

Judgment is still judgment, even if you know (which is to say *believe*) you are right.

Just remember that whether you are a fish, giraffe, or reticulated python, you may accidentally take on the role of a well-meaning monkey if you are given enough motivation from an exasperating armadillo. But the true task is to remain open to their unique genius regardless of how it does not sync up with your own.

At the end of the day, it still all comes down to this:

"Love your neighbor as yourself."

\- Mark 12:31

Let's try to cut everyone, and I mean *everyone*, no matter how difficult it may be, the same slack we would want to be cut ourselves.

COLLABORATION REQUIRES OTHERS

As I said, you can't do this alone. We are here together at this time in this situation for a reason. "We" means all of us.

When someone gets cast in a play, nobody checks first to make sure that everyone in the cast is going to like everybody else. You know that you have to depend on each other, so you find a way to work together, even if the people you are cast with are not the same people you would hang out with by choice.

You may not like the other characters in the production that is your life, but if you come at it from the soul perspective, they are just like you. They too are a soul that came here to play a character and are doing their level best to understand and manage their own relationship with themselves. You now have an advantage in that you understand what they are going through on the metaphorical level of the plane and the pilot, so take it easy. Embrace them all. They are all on a journey of their own making, just like you are, and you are in their production, just like they are in yours.

So be kind to your fellow players.

*"Your life is like a play with several acts.
Some of the characters who enter have short roles to play,
others, much larger. Some are villains and others are good
guys. But all of them are necessary; otherwise, they
wouldn't be in the play. Embrace them all, and move on
to the next act. "*

\- Wayne Dyer

CHAPTER 11
GETTING TO PRODUCTION

"I think of life itself now as a wonderful play that I've written for myself, and so my purpose is to have the utmost fun playing my part."

\- **Shirley MacLaine**

THE METAPHORICAL QUIBBLE

Let's return one last time to the quote that inspired the guiding metaphor of this entire book.

> *"All the world's a stage and all the men and women merely players."*

> - William Shakespeare, *As You Like It* (2.7.138)

And I suspect you won't be surprised at this point that I can't help but want to emphasize one word and quibble with another.

Let's start with the quibble.

"…all the men and women **merely** players." In the context of the play from which it comes, the character of Jaques is a bit (OK, *a lot*) bummed and therefore uses the word "merely" to describe in a diminishing way the role of human beings.

But yeah, merely means "nothing more than, just, or only" according to Mr. Webster. I think we've pretty much established that in the context of the world as we know it (apologies to the melancholy Jaques), there is nothing *merely* about us as players in any use of the word.

We've gone into quite a deep dive about what it means to be a player on the great stage of life, and since the aspect of us that is the player is our soulful true self, there's nothing *merely* about it.

And neither are we nothing more than, just, or only players.

YES, AND... - ING THE METAPHOR

Yes, you are the player, playing this character on the great stage of life, **and**... you are also the playwright of the masterpiece you call your life. We are not *just* the player, playing the character.

We are each playing a character in a story of our own creation.

Yeah, OK. So it's a cool concept and all, but let's really drink that in.

Being the playwright means that not only have we created our character, but we have also created all the other characters, all the given circumstances, and everything that is in our lives. All of it. We are choosing what to create and choosing what to keep.

Your choices are everything!

We are deciding, moment to moment, not just our own thoughts, feelings, and the actions we take, but the people, places, and things that we choose to keep as a part of our story. It is all what becomes the production of our life. If it's here in our life, it's because we have written it into the fabric of our experience.

If we did not write it, it would not be here.

THE META IN OUR METAPHOR

For most of us, even when we have accepted the metaphor of being players in the role of a lifetime on the great stage of life, we still perceive our lives as being created by forces *outside* us rather than being created by the brilliant, powerful force *inside* us.

We still relegate the rest of our experience, the play itself, the other characters, and all the other production elements to the Universe. We tell ourselves and each other that we are not responsible for our story and that we did not create our circumstances.

We make the Universe the playwright in order to have that default ego-appeasing answer to all our *whys*. But in truth, in our meta-metaphor, the Universe is clearly the Producer.

In the theater, the producer is the one that puts the production in motion and controls all the resources available to that production. Without the producer, there would be no production. The producer is the source of supply of all the necessary elements to put on a good production on the stage and in life.

Sounds like the Universe to me.

THE BEST PRODUCER EVER!!!

There is not a theater company, an actor, or a director in the world that would not feel blessed beyond words to find that they had a producer with unlimited resources that was completely willing to fund, support, and supply anything they wanted to create on their stage. If a company of actors were told that they could play anything, create anything, be, do, and have whatever they needed to fulfill the characters they chose to create and the story they chose to tell? Oh, baby! They would be overjoyed. You might even say *blissful* (see what we did there?)

Unfortunately for all those actually in the theater, there is no theater company in the world that has a producer willing to say that. Because all producers in the theater are actually humans and, like all humans, they believe in a limit to resources.

But good news! Your producer on the great stage of life has no such belief. The Universe knows it is limitless! That means our production, our life, has limitless resources that are being offered to us unconditionally! Is it time for a happy dance yet?

AND IF THAT WERE NOT ENOUGH

In addition to being player, character, and playwright in the production of your life, you hold one more job as well: that of Director.

The director's job in the theater is to act as the unifying visionary for the entire production. They establish the vision and they guide the entire ensemble of the production on the path of bringing that vision to fruition.

So that part of you that is the director (your consciousness) gets to hold the vision and do the work to develop, nurture, problem solve, collaborate, and guide the production (your life) through an evolutionary process of learning and discovery to bring it to the stage.

HOLDING THE VISION

About 20 years ago, I was the artistic director of The New Heritage Theatre Company. Anthony Hopkins was the Honorary Patron of the company and my mentor during those years.

One day, as he and I were climbing over piles of literal trash to look through a building that we were hoping would one day house the theater company, Tony said, *"Do you see it?"*

The look on my face must have told him I didn't understand, because he smiled and repeated, *"Do you see it? Do you see it completed? In the future? Can you see it when you go to bed at night and first thing when you wake up in the morning? Can you see it?"*

"Yes," I said.

"Good," he said. *"Then it's already done. It already exists out there. We just have to be smart enough to catch up to it."*

As both playwright and director, this is what you are doing. You are determining what story you wish to tell, establishing the vision, and bringing it into being by being smart enough and persistent enough to *catch up to it*.

LIVING THE DREAM

Let's imagine for a moment that you are dreaming. You ready? In this dream…

You are a tremendously successful and skilled actor.

And you are perfectly cast in your
role of a lifetime.

And this entire production is tailor-made
for you!

And you are the playwright as well!

And, if that were not enough, you are
also the director of this production!!!

And you have the most fabulous, generous, loving, gracious producer in the Universe!!!!!
(pun intended)

OK, newsflash. That *is* your life.

That's what is happening.

OPENING NIGHT

In life, we often get caught in a perpetual state of getting ready to get ready. But in the theater, opening night is opening night, and being ready is not optional. It's just the way it is.

If we waited for the tickets to be sold and the theater to be full before we started rehearsal, there would be a lot of angry people with tired butts waiting in those seats by the time we ever got around to doing anything. But that is the way we treat life.

We act like we can stay in a perpetual rehearsal if we decide to, like we don't actually have to perform. But I've got news for us! We're on! We are performing! Wait, how did that happen?!

Oh yeah, we were born!!!!!

That's right folks! This production of our lives started the day we started our life. Imagine that?

This production is not waiting for you to decide you're ready before it takes off. That's the ol' ego that thinks it's in control again. And if you're here reading this book, odds are, you've played quite a few scenes of your life's production by now.

Question is, did you play them with all the awareness and wonder they deserve? Did you show up with your imagination engaged, having done your character analysis, ready for the improv, offering and accepting spontaneously, finding the love, aware of your objectives, making specific choices, and embracing your obstacles?

…probably not.

ALL THE WORLD

OK, that brings us back to the one word in the quote that I need to emphasize: **all**. Yep, that's the one. *All* the world's a stage. You're not getting ready to go on stage, YOU'RE ON. And all the world, all of *your* world, every moment of your existence since the moment of your birth is the performance of a lifetime.

And then the collaboration begins. But the collaboration is not just us with others. The essential collaboration is between us and ourselves.

We need each aspect of ourselves to join in the vision, embrace it, and set about living it with complete awareness of our player self, showing up as our character, playwright, and director.

You don't have to step onto the stage. You are already there.

What you do have to do is step into the light and fully accept *all* responsibility for this production and *all* that you bring to it and *all* that it brings to the world in, as, and through you.

ACTING AS IF

There is a concept that evolved from Konstantin Stanislovski, who was the director of the Moscow Art Theatre in the early 20th century and the father of modern acting technique. Stanislavski introduced the concept of the "if."

"When I give a genuine answer to the "if", then I do something, I am living my own personal life. At moments like that there is no character. Only me."

- Konstantin Stanislavski

The concept of the "if," which has also come to be known as the magic what if, behaving as if, or acting as if, is simply the process by which an actor asks themselves, *"What if [fill in the blank] were true? What would I do?"*

As Stanislavski says, once you have a genuine answer to the if, you know how to show up authentically in that moment and act or behave as if what you imagine to be true *is*.

That is what actors are doing when they are said to be behaving truthfully. They are behaving as though the thing that they imagine to be true *is* true. Remember what Mr. Meisner said:

"Acting is behaving truthfully under imaginary circumstances."

PERSISTENCE MEETS PASSION

When the lighting guy comes up and tells you about a problem, you don't just throw up your hands and say, *"Well then, I'm going home and I'm watching reruns of Gilligan's Island!"* The lighting problem is an offer masquerading as an obstacle. And no offense to Gilligan's

Island, but in this case (you guessed it) that would be blocking.

Instead you say, *"OK, what's the problem and how can we either work with it or work around it?"* The key here is that you keep working toward the vision. Hold the vision. That's the job of the director.

You problem solve. You collaborate.

Because before you start rehearsal, the resources are committed. In other words, **you** are committed. You have a vision and you hold to that vision.

But it's not about knowing exactly what that journey is going to look like. You're taking the journey as it comes.

When you start toward an opening date in the theater, it's a done deal. It will happen. Because all theater folk know what we sometimes forget in life: if you persist, it is impossible not to succeed.

And in life, just doing it, sticking with it, continuing to offer, accept, and follow your bliss makes success inevitable.

It just may not look exactly like the original idea or vision that came to you. In fact, it NEVER does! It's **better**.

Bumps will occur. Challenges will occur. But they are not the focus, they are the obstacles. They are the inspiration. Just don't get confused by focusing your energy and attention on what you don't want to have happen.

Remember, you have to focus on what you want, not on what you don't want.

THIS IS NOT A TEST

Our life is not a test. You are playing this character because you chose to. You are learning and growing and evolving for the sheer fun of learning and growing and evolving.

Life is what we came here to do. Life is not what we came here to become *worthy* to do.

We are not living to become worthy of the life we desire, but rather we are here to live a life that is worthy of us.

We've already got the part!!! We've got the job!!!!!

Isn't it amazing?! So much is offered to you by your soulful self. So much is offered to you by the Universe. It's time to "Yes, and…" your life. **YES** to all that is **AND** all that is yet to be.

WHAT'S IN A MINDSET

Getting to production on the stage and in life begins with a vision and a commitment to that vision.

There is so much talk about "mindset" these days. Thought leaders talk constantly about the need for a positive mindset in order to manifest or bring about your "best life."

But if the *mind* that you are trying to *set* is the director inside you, then mindset is simply the commitment to the vision your inner director or consciousness has set.

So, with your imagination fully engaged, think like a director for a second. Explore that vision, set it in your mind, lock it in, and visualize it.

Then go to the best producer ever and ask specifically for all the elements you need, knowing that you will receive them unconditionally, in order to get this production produced at its best.

Engage your playwright to be creating the story rather than just acting as a scribe and writing down whatever the characters improvise. Get a good script and be willing to rewrite whenever necessary.

Remember that your director self is responsible for holding the vision consistently, bringing all the practical elements together, and developing the story with the playwright.

Do the deep dive into the character that you are playing. Find the love and use that as a roadmap for the choices that will best serve the story you are trying to tell.

Having the proper mindset is about staying in alignment with your vision and then manifesting results by thinking, deciding and acting as if it's already true.

THE PERFECT PRODUCTION

There isn't one.

A production in any venue, by any company, will have imperfections, because no matter how much rehearsal and planning you do, there is always that element of improvisation. Meaning there are always things that will happen that are unexpected.

The imperfections and the skill with which they are handled are what make the experience of live theater hold the level of vitality and in-the-moment excitement that it does. Each performance, each production, and each portrayal is a unique event. People don't walk out of the theater — whether audience, cast, or crew — and say, *"That was perfect!"* They say, *"That was exciting!"* *"That was amazing!"* *"That was so funny!"* *"That was so sad!"* *"That was so exhilarating!"* *"That was wonderful!"*

But never, *"That was perfect."*

Perfectionism is a creation of the protective personality. It's a monkey concept. The closer you get to the perfect climbing of the tree, the safer you are. You are safer from criticism, you are safer from disappointment, and you are safer from having to try anything else.

Oxford Languages defines perfection like this:

- having all the required or desirable elements, qualities, or characteristics; as good as it is possible to be
- absolute; complete
- completely free from faults or defects, or as close to such a condition as possible

But let me ask you this. How would we know perfect if we didn't know what it wasn't? How would we have something to strive for if we didn't understand what it felt like to have something fail?

Each person is their own perfect. Your perfect contains your bliss. Your perfect is the way that brings you joy. Your perfect is not the one that someone else chooses for you.

A giraffe in a tree may have experienced perfect according to the monkey. But if the giraffe doesn't feel perfect, experience their bliss, or if finding the love for them would require them to be standing on the ground, then it's not *their* perfect.

Your perfect is unique. Just as your genius, your creativity, and your bliss is. They are all *yours*.

They are yours to discover, yours to choose, yours to embrace, yours to accept, yours to offer, yours to use to make other folks look good, and yours to use to overcome obstacles.

It's not a question of whether or not you deserve it. You are it. When your soul chose this life the Universe poured the entire sea of infinite possibilities into your very being. If that's not perfect, I don't know what is!

Now it's just a matter of acting on and offering the perfect.

SHOW DON'T TELL

When I am directing actors and they bring an idea to me, my immediate answer is, *"Let's try it. Show me."* Because there is no way we can make the decision about how to play a moment on the stage by just thinking about it or discussing it. We still have to see it in action to decide. We "put it on its feet" and then we play with the idea and tweak it and finally come to a decision and choose what will work best for that moment, for the story, and for the production as a whole.

And so it is in life.

Everything in the theater — acting, directing, and writing — is an evolutionary process.

And so it is in life.

And the evolution doesn't occur by just thinking about it or feeling about it or talking about it. You have to take action.

And so it is in —

OMG! In this moment, right now, as I'm finishing this book, I just found another "in acting, as in life…"

I just realized that my definition of creativity in Chapter 2 is also a detailed description of a successful production on the stage *and* on the great stage of life!

Creativity and Theater and Life are each:

The conscious and deliberate evolutionary process of developing a thought or thoughts in the imagination and then taking action on those thoughts in order to manifest change, alter perception, enhance understanding, or to bring into being something as yet unrealized in our awareness or physical reality.

Wow! That's so cool!

So I guess we can come right back to where we started.

You are a unique creative genius with a passion and purpose that you came here to share.

So please do.

It's simple:

> Accept everything as an offer.
> When in doubt, offer!
> If in doubt, you are probably blocking.

And just remember that if it's in your life, whatever it is, you meant it to be here, so find the love. You are not just the scribe, you are the playwright. This is your story. This is your production. This is your life.

So whatever the question…

The answer is you.

> *"This above all: to thine own self be true."*

> \- William Shakespeare, *Hamlet* (1.3.564)

ACKNOWLEDGEMENTS

I must first and foremost acknowledge all of my students, from 1986 till now, who it has been my privilege and honor to play with and to challenge. Thank you for the honor and the fun.

To all the actors, directors, playwrights, and theater practitioners who have played in the playground with me over all these decades: thank you, thank you, thank you. After all the decades of "playing," there are far too many of you to mention individually, but please know that I hold you all in my heart.

I have had a great many teachers, mentors, and coaches in my theatrical life over the past five decades. It is the education, inspiration, mentorship, encouragement, and glorious opportunities that I received from these people that provided the fertile ground to develop my ideas, techniques, beliefs, passions, and practices as a director, actor, writer, teacher, and creativity specialist. Many I have mentioned in these pages and others perhaps not, but every individual on this list has impacted my career and my life in ways both profound and perfect: Casey Kizziah, Mario Siletti, James Tripp, Lisa Jacobson, Peter Lobdell, Joan Evans, Robert Perillo, Eric Forsythe, Miriam Gilbert, Giles Block, Roddy Maude Roxby, Ken Campbell, Helen Chadwick, Anthony Naylor, Anthony Cornish, Bardy Thomas, my theater dad Dr. Robert Ericson (Doc), Dr. Charles Lauterbach, Steve Buss, Frank Heise, Fred Norman, George Borchers, Joe Gratton, Victoria Holloway, Allen Grunerud, Kim Mara, Art Borreca, Rick Scott, Jane Armitage, Alan MacVey, Sherry Kramer, Eva Le Gallienne (thank you Eloise Armen), Uta Hagen, Hector Elizondo, the wise and wonderful Anthony Hopkins (Tony), and my dear cherished friend, mentor, and theater mom Olympia Dukakis (Oly).

And to the one teacher with whom I never had any personal interaction but who inspired me over 30 years ago (via Ken, Roddy, and his brilliant book Impro) to see spontaneity and imagination in remarkable new ways: bless you, Keith Johnstone.

I would also like to acknowledge and thank the people who have been my greatest partners in the creative dance of life, the people who have helped me explore and express my own unique creative genius in my personal and spiritual life. First and foremost, thank you to my daughters Brit, Andi, Ria, and Shell. You girls are my greatest teachers, my greatest loves, my besties, and my greatest motivators. Thank you for allowing me to be your Mom, the greatest role I could ever hope to play. I love you all so much. Special thanks to Shell for co-parenting and co-creating with me for all these years. You're my rock. Bless you, Bear. And special thanks as well to my bonus dot and daughter-in-love Annie. I am so blessed to have you in my life. Thanks for letting me be your "other Mom," it's an honor. And thanks to all my bonus kids and kids-in-love: Christopher, Robin, Kelly (Fuzzy), Maia, Jessy, and Tori. Huggies and lovies.

My life partner Rex… wow. The list of beautiful, wonderful things that I've learned from you, and experienced because of you, seems endless. Thank you for being, my Angel, my cryptic wise sage, and for the simple joys and boundless adventure of taking the journey together.

To my Mother, Lottie, and my Dad, Leon, who loved, allowed, and supported the expression of me from the very beginning, I love you forever and I miss you every day.

And thank you to the great miracle ladies in my life. The coaches, friends, guides, mentors, and miracle sisters who have shared my journey of wisdom seeking over the years. I am certain I would not be who I am in this moment were it not for the impact of the wisdom and wonder you have shared. Thank you Marci Schimoff, Debra Poneman, Leila Reyes, Dr. Sue Morter, Lisa Garr, Mary Morissey, Frances, "Mama" Stephanie Downing, Neicer Rae, Ilene Leasure, Jennifer Dunn, Carla Leafty, Shaun Cox Leonard, Katie Preston, Pirie Grossman, Sue Donnellan, my original IC Miracles Group: Carol, Sondra, Rebecca, and Carla, and all my miracle sisters over the years.

To Dene. Thanks Bud, for kicking the ideas around, for playing devil's advocate, for all your help, for always listening, and for always taking it seriously. And to Miguel, thank you so much for sharing your beautiful creative genius. Blessings, my friend.

And to the team of five people, my editors, publishers, and publicists who have been instrumental in helping me bring this book to fruition, bless you ladies:

Viki Winterton. Thank you for your wisdom and generous spirit. You are so missed.

Pamela Murphy. Thank you for your enthusiasm, steadfast support, and your exquisite patience.

Michele Chynoweth. Your faith in me and in this book blew into my life like a lovely breeze of fresh crisp air and re-energized the whole process. I am forever grateful.

Michelle Oneida. What can I say? If it weren't for you telling me to please put all of this into a book, I don't know if I ever would have. As an editor, your ability to see the big picture and instantly cut to the chase is astounding. Your genius never ceases to amaze me. Thanks for just simply getting me in a way that no one else ever has. Your wisdom, your imagination, your kindness, and your playful creativity are a blessing to my head and to my heart.

And finally, Vicki Anne Crane. There is really no way to encapsulate or overstate your impact on this book. I simply could not have done this without you. To say that I am grateful for you and all your hard work is a massive understatement. Thank you for your patience, your persistence, your brilliance, and your geeky love of grammar and organization! You are amazing!

SUGGESTED READING

Below you will find a smattering of books that I enjoy. This is an eclectic mix of books on acting, spirituality, self-help, Shakespeare, and even a novel or two. They are in alphabetical order by author because it's hard for me to prioritize them in any other way. This list could easily have been 3 times as long, but I decided to stop here so that my publisher would not abandon me. Have fun.

- Stella Adler, *The Technique of Acting* (1988)
- Marc Allen, *The Ten Percent Solution: Simple Steps to Improve Our Lives and Our World Paperback* (2002)
- Marc Allen, *The Millionaire Course* (2003)
- Richard Back, *Illusions: The Adventures of a Reluctant Messiah* (2001)
- Sylvan Barnet (editor), *The Complete Signet Classic Shakespeare* (1972)
- John Barton, *Playing Shakespeare* (2001)
- Giles Block & Mark Rylance, *Speaking the Speech: An Actor's Guide to Shakespeare* (2013)
- Harold Bloom, *Shakespeare: The Invention of the Human* (1998)
- Oscar Lee Brownstein, *Strategies of Drama: The Experience of Form* (1991)
- Joseph Campbell, *The Hero with a Thousand Faces* (1949)
- Joseph Campbell & Bill Moyers, *The Power of Myth* (1991)
- Michael Chekhov, *On the Technique of Acting* (1953)
- Deepak Chopra, *The Seven Spiritual Laws of Success: A Practical Guide to the Fulfillment of Your Dreams* (1994)

- Mike Dooley, *Infinite Possibilities: The Art of Living Your Dreams* (2001)
- Wayne Dyer, *Wishes Fulfilled* (2012)
- Emmet Fox, *The Sermon on the Mount* (1934)
- Uta Hagen, *Respect for Acting* (1973)
- Thich Nhat Hanh, *The Miracle of Mindfulness* (1975)
- Keith Johnstone, *Impro: Improvisation and the Theatre* (1979)
- Sanford Meisner, *On Acting* (1987)
- Mary Morrisey, *Building Your Field of Dreams* (1996)
- Dr. Sue Morter, *The Energy Codes: The 7-Step System to Awaken Your Spirit, Heal Your Body, and Live Your Best Life* (2019)
- Arnold M. Patent, *You Can Have It All* (1984)
- Don Miguel Ruiz, *The Four Agreements: A Practical Guide to Personal Freedom* (1997)
- Antoine de Saint-Exupéry, *The Little Prince* (1943)
- Marci Shimoff, *Happy for No Reason: 7 Steps to Being Happy from the Inside Out* (2009)
- Marci Shimoff, *Love for No Reason: 7 Steps to Creating a Life of Unconditional Love* (2010)
- Eckhart Tolle, *The Power of Now: A Guide to Spiritual Enlightenment* (2004)